A MURDER H
ARRAN(

A Ghost Story in Three Acts

by

EMLYN WILLIAMS

SAMUEL   FRENCH

LONDON
NEW YORK   TORONTO   SYDNEY   HOLLYWOOD

FOR AMATEUR PRODUCTION ENQUIRIES

UNITED KINGDOM AND WORLD EXCLUDING NORTH AMERICA

plays@SamuelFrench-London.co.uk

020 7255 4302/01

Each title is subject to availability from Samuel French,

depending upon country of performance.

A MURDER HAS BEEN ARRANGED

First presented by the Repertory Players, at the Strand Theatre, London, on Sunday, 9th November 1930, with the following cast of characters:

MISS GROZE	*Ann Codrington*
CAVENDISH	*Guy Pelham Boulton*
MRS WRAGG	*Amy Veness*
JIMMY NORTH	*Whitmore Humphreys*
BEATRICE JASPER	*Margaretta Scott*
MRS ARTHUR, her mother	*Violet Farebrother*
SIR CHARLES JASPER	*Wilfrid Caithness*
MAURICE MULLINS	*Henry Kendall*
A WOMAN	*Veronica Turleigh*

Presented for a London run by the Daniel Mayer Company, at the St James's Theatre, on Wednesday, 26th November 1930, with the following changes of cast:

CAVENDISH	*John Cheatle*
MRS ARTHUR	*Viola Compton*
SIR CHARLES JASPER	*J. H. Roberts*

On both occasions the play was produced by the Author

The Scene of the Play: *Here*—that is to say, the stage of the St James's Theatre London

The Time of the Play: *Now*—that is to say, between 8.15 and 11.15 on the night of Wednesday, 26th November, 1930, Sir Jasper's fortieth birthday

There will be two intervals of ten minutes each

BEFORE THE PLAY

The overture is played by a small dance band, and consists of lively topical fox-trots.

THE HOUSE-LIGHTS *go out just on twenty to nine and the band attacks a new tune, very loud and very fast. Suddenly a woman in evening dress dashes through the parting of the* CURTAIN.

MISS GROZE. Stop!

(*A dead pause*)

THE BAND CONDUCTOR. What's the matter?

MISS GROZE. I'm frightened. . . . I can't stand another minute alone on this stage! (*Calling*) Mrs Wragg! Please—please lift up this curtain!

A pause. The CURTAIN *rises on——*

A MURDER HAS BEEN ARRANGED

ACT I

The stage is very dimly lit; the most prominent objects are an armchair and sofa draped in dust-sheets.

MISS GROZE. Mrs Wragg! Please, please turn on the lights. Λrs Wragg, I'm frightened! (*She sinks into the armchair. She is about thirty; pretty in a hard way, and very smartly dressed*) This silence—it's awful.

THE BAND CONDUCTOR. Now, now, Miss Groze, pull yourself together! (*He is a pleasant, matter-of-fact man; the personification of the ordinary*)

MISS GROZE. It's all very well for you, there are seven of you, and you can always play some jazz to cheer yourselves up, but I —honestly, Mr Cavendish, it's driving me crazy . . .

(*The telephone rings on the stage*)

CAVENDISH. What's that?

MISS GROZE (*taking off the receiver*) Oh, I'm not frightened of the telephone. That's human. And it's contact with the outside world . . . Yes, this is the St James's Theatre . . . The *Daily Mail?* . . . This *is* Sir Charles Jasper's secretary speaking . . . An interview? No, I'm afraid nobody at all is allowed in the theatre tonight, Sir Charles is very strict . . . Yes, yes, I'm speaking from the stage now, Sir Charles had an extension put in yesterday from the stage door . . . Yes, you may use that . . . Yes, yes, the orchestra has just played and the curtain has just been raised . . . Yes, exactly like a real play, in accordance with Sir Charles's orders. . . . Yes, the theatre is quite empty. It's been empty over a week, it's closed for cleaning. You may use that . . . (*Suddenly apprehensive*) What? . . . No—there is no evidence as yet that the theatre is—haunted . . . Good-bye. (*She hangs up, and stares in front of her*)

CAVENDISH. Haunted . . .

MISS GROZE. Oh, don't . . .

CAVENDISH. It's a curious sort of a word—haunted . . .

(MISS GROZE *shivers involuntarily*)

Now, now, Miss Groze!

MISS GROZE. I'm all right . . .

CAVENDISH. You're afraid.

MISS GROZE. I'm not afraid! Afraid of what, anyway?

CAVENDISH. Well, how can I tell what we're all afraid of, till it actually happens?

MISS GROZE (*rising and advancing to the footlights*) So you're afraid—too?

CAVENDISH. Well, n-no . . . But I don't mind admitting I'd sooner be at home by the fire than in St James's Theatre tonight! It'd be a bit better if there was a regular performance going on—but to be asked to play dance music at half-past eight at night in an empty theatre! Just you and us here, and four other people!

MISS GROZE (*turning her back on him*) If Sir Charles chooses to pay you for it . . .

CAVENDISH. Why did those two maids leave here so suddenly this afternoon?

(MISS GROZE *starts, and sits in the armchair, making a pretence at self-possession*)

MISS GROZE. Nothing out of the ordinary can possibly happen. Nothing ever has in your life or my life so far, why should it start tonight?

CAVENDISH. The only thing to do is to wait and see. It might be—anything.

MISS GROZE. Anything . . . (*She opens a drawer in the table beside her*)

CAVENDISH. What's that?

MISS GROZE. A revolver. Mrs Arthur's . . . "Just in case," she said. (*Putting it back*) Oh, I wish that Wragg woman would turn on some lights! (*Rising and coming down to him again*) Won't you play?

CAVENDISH. I think we've done enough rehearsing for the moment, don't you? I hope you were listening to us just now?

MISS GROZE. I think Sir Charles'll be satisfied.

CAVENDISH (*rising*) Right! Well, boys, what about that game of poker?

MISS GROZE. Oh, don't go!

CAVENDISH. Now, Miss Groze, don't you be silly. We'll be under the stage if you want us! Why don't you go and sit in one of the dressing-rooms?

MISS GROZE. It's worse there. The passages are so dark.

CAVENDISH. Well, wait and see, that's all I can say. Boys, I think I was winning, wasn't I?

(*They clatter under the stage. Silence. MISS GROZE stands over the footlights with her back to the auditorium*)

MISS GROZE. Haunted . . . Oh . . .

(*Full stage lights are suddenly turned on. She gives a cry of relief. In the following description of the scene, and throughout the play, "left" and "right" are taken as the left and right of a person on the stage facing the auditorium.*)

The stage is occupied by an interior set, plain to the point of austerity, with pale green-grey walls and black carpeting. C back, a large alcove, reached by two shallow steps, with black curtains, meeting in the middle and working by hand, which are open at the moment; it contains tall windows silhouetted against a blue-lit backing. On the right of the alcove, an immense archway. There is no backing behind it; merely the dim wilderness of an empty theatre. In the R wall, up stage, a double door opening on. Between the set and the footlights, on each side, a narrow opening giving access to the wings—the left opening and the right opening.

The furniture is rich and plain. In the alcove, at all armchair. Down stage R, a narrow refectory table, almost at right angles to the footlights, with a low candelabra, and supper laid for four; a stool on each side of it. Down stage L, an armchair and sofa, with, between them, a small low table with a telephone, a book, and cigarettes and matches. Down stage L, against the wall, a low pouffe. Against the L wall, a low sideboard with decanter, glasses, and soda-water siphon)

MRS WRAGG (*in the wings*) Is that all right, miss?

MISS GROZE. Yes, yes.

(*A pause. She takes off the dust-sheets.*

MRS WRAGG comes in from the right of the archway. She is a cook, fat, middle-aged, and dressed in stiff alpaca with an apron. By nature a kind soul, she is at the moment bristling with dislike of Miss Groze. MISS GROZE hands her the dust-sheets. She sniffs and takes no notice)

Why couldn't you turn the lights on before?

MRS WRAGG. Couldn't find the switches, miss. D'you want me to blow the whole blooming place up? I nearly brained myself pulling up this blooming curtain.

MISS GROZE. That will do, thank you. Lady Jasper wants to know immediately what preparations you're making for supper tonight. Quickly, please!

MRS WRAGG. And Sir Charles Jasper wants to know immediately if the curtain's up and the lights are on and the band 'as rehearsed. Double up now!

(*MISS GROZE gives her a look of impotent fury, and walks to the archway. She hesitates, as if frightened of what is beyond. MRS WRAGG shrugs her shoulders, and makes to lead the way herself. She wavers*)

MISS GROZE. We—we'll go up together.

MRS WRAGG (*in a whisper*) Are you frightened of something —too?

(*They go out to the right of the archway. A pause. Footsteps clattering in the right wings.*

JIMMY NORTH enters by the right opening and nearly falls over the footlights. He is a good-looking, boyish young man. He looks round the stage apprehensively, sees the telephone and has a sudden inspiration. He crosses to it, listens if anyone is coming, and lifts the receiver. In the same second he realizes it is a stage telephone, and again almost immediately hears a voice at the other end)

JIMMY (*surprised*) I say, this telephone isn't really a telephone, is it? . . . Oh, sorry, miss—you see, I'm on the stage. . . . No, not an actor! . . . No, it'd take too long to explain, will you give me Putney o-nine-o-five. (*He looks round again, peers cautiously into the orchestra pit, and looks round the theatre in wonder*) Hallo, is that you, Keith? Look here, Keith, in a few minutes will you ring up the St James's Theatre—er—(*looking at the number*) Gerrard three-nine-double-four—and say you're the *Daily Express* . . . What? . . . No, I know you're not the *Daily Express*, but *say* you are! And say you're sending round a reporter named—er—I think I'll call myself—Simon Richardson . . . No, I can't explain now . . .

(MISS GROZE *stands in the archway watching him, holding some table napkins. He sees her*)

No, I'm afraid this is *not* the Shaftesbury Hospital for Diseases of the Eye, good-bye. (*He hangs up, coughs, lifts his hat, smiles, and wanders down beyond the sofa, extremely ill-at-ease*) You know, something really ought to be done about these wrong numbers. It is sickening, isn't it?

MISS GROZE. I'm afraid I haven't had the privilege . . .

JIMMY. Er—Richardson—er—Simon Richardson. The telephone rang. I answered it for you.

MISS GROZE (*coldly*) Thank you.

JIMMY. Have I the pleasure of speaking to Miss Groze, Sir Charles Jasper's private secretary?

MISS GROZE. You have.

JIMMY (*beaming*) Really!

(MISS GROZE *stares at him*)

(*His smile fading*) Oh, really. I say, is this really the stage?

MISS GROZE. It is.

JIMMY. You know, Miss Groze, I've never been on a stage before. Isn't it a lark?

MISS GROZE. Is it?

JIMMY. Oh. Perhaps you're right. May I sit down?

(*No answer.* MISS GROZE *sits in the armchair*)

I feel perhaps I'd be more at my ease—sitting down.

(*No answer*)

(*Sitting on the sofa*) Thank you.

MISS GROZE. Don't you think you might be still more at your ease walking down Piccadilly?

JIMMY. More at my ease walking down—oh . . . Do—do you really think so, Miss Groze?

MISS GROZE. I'm afraid you're wasting both your own time and mine, Mr—er——

JIMMY (*lost*) Er—Symonson. Er—Richard—er—Symonson.

MISS GROZE. I thought you said your name was Simon Richardson?

JIMMY (*still more lost*) Oh . . . Did I? I mean—well, I can't have done, if my name's the other one, can I?

MISS GROZE. Which other one?

JIMMY (*completely at sea*) Why—er—Richard Symonson. (*He grins at her ingratiatingly and takes out his cigarette-case*)

MISS GROZE. Has your mother ever told you you have a charming smile?

JIMMY (*encouraged*) Well, no . . . Why?

MISS GROZE. Because you look as if she had.

JIMMY. Oh. Won't you smoke?

MISS GROZE. It isn't allowed on the stage.

JIMMY. Jolly sensible, too. (*Striking a match*) Might put the whole theatre on fire. You know, Miss Groze, I find a cigarette's wonderful when the brain's tired.

MISS GROZE. Whose brain? (*Rising*) Look here, this is going a bit too far. First of all you walk in here without so much as a by-your-leave . . .

JIMMY. The stage door was open and there was nobody there to give me a by-your-leave . . .

MISS GROZE. There's no doorkeeper here tonight. You ought to have waited.

JIMMY. Ah, but you see I have an impetuous nature. And I walked down here. And I met you.

MISS GROZE. I'd be quite justified in ringing up the police . . .

JIMMY (*rising ingratiatingly*) Oh, you'd never do that!

MISS GROZE. No.

JIMMY (*smiling*) Thank you.

MISS GROZE. I'd be quite justified in ringing up the police, if you didn't look perfectly harmless.

JIMMY. Oh!

MISS GROZE. Well?

JIMMY. As a matter of fact, Miss Groze, I—I'm a (*producing a notebook*) a—reporter. I heard that yesterday Sir Charles rang up the owner of this theatre and asked him permission to live on the stage here until tomorrow—(*reading from his notebook*) in an interior set left over from the last play running here.

MISS GROZE. And you've heard that the first step in interviews is to vamp the lady secretaries? (*She crosses to the supper-table and puts the napkins in their places*)

JIMMY (*following her round the table*) Well—try to, you know. You see, Miss Groze . . .

Miss Groze. Quarter to nine at night is no time for a Press interview. Good evening.

(*The telephone rings. She pushes him on one side and answers it*)

Yes. . . . This is the St James's Theatre. . . . The *Daily Express*? . . . What name is it, please? . . . Simon Richardson? . . . (*Taken aback*) Oh, certainly. . . . Good-bye. . . .

(Jimmy *sits beside the supper-table with a broad grin*)

What *is* your name, Richard Symonson or Simon Richardson?

Jimmy. Why—er—(*lost again*) the one he said, of course. You see, Miss Groze, I write for two different papers under two different names, that's why I'm liable to get so mixed up. . . . Well?

Miss Groze (*producing notes*) I can only give you the information that was passed on to the others. I have just three minutes.

Jimmy. I already have down that Sir Charles Jasper is the author of that famous book, *The Occult Through the Ages*, and has amassed nearly fifty thousand pounds from Jasper Washing Powder.

Miss Groze. His uncle, Anthony Jasper, made a will in his favour, but in his youth Sir Charles was not at all strong . . .

Jimmy (*writing*) Sir Charles—enjoyed—poor health.

Miss Groze. And the doctors were afraid he would never reach middle-age. For this reason the will states that if Sir Charles is alive on his fortieth birthday, that is, today, Wednesday, November the twenty-sixth, nineteen-thirty, at eleven p.m., the hour of his birth, he inherits the two million pounds left by his uncle.

Jimmy. Two million . . . Nought . . . Nought . . . Nought. I think I'd better spell it.

Miss Groze. If, on the contrary, Sir Charles were to die before tonight, the money would revert to his only living relative, a Maurice Mullins, whose whereabouts are unknown.

Jimmy. If—on the contrary—Sir Charles dies before eleven o'clock tonight . . .

Miss Groze. I said "If Sir Charles *were* to die."

Jimmy. Ah, but you never know!

Miss Groze. It's nearly nine now, and Sir Charles does not suffer from heart failure.

Jimmy. You—never—know! It sounds much more exciting, anyway . . . If Sir Charles dies before eleven o'clock tonight, this fortune will be—I before E except after C, received—by Maurice Mullins.

Miss Groze. Haven't you ever heard of shorthand?

Jimmy. My longhand's really awfully good!

(Miss Groze *turns away from him. The void beyond the archway at the back of the stage seems to frighten her*)

Maurice Mullins . . .

(He looks up at her. She collects herself abruptly and returns his look)

MISS GROZE. What's the matter with you now?

JIMMY. Nothing—except you look rather frightened of something.

MISS GROZE. Go on with that.

JIMMY. Oh . . . Any information about the party?

MISS GROZE. At ten o'clock Sir Charles is having a little family supper on the stage, but the guests for the party itself will start arriving about half-past eleven.

JIMMY. One more thing, Miss Groze . . . Could you confirm the rumour that the party is to be in fancy dress?

MISS GROZE. The party is in fancy dress. Revue costumes, from the wardrobe here, representing Ghosts of History.

JIMMY. Ghosts of History?

MISS GROZE. Such as Mary Queen of Scots, Francis Drake, Queen Elizabeth, and . . .

JIMMY. And Crippen.

(Far away, very solemnly, a church clock strikes nine. They listen)

MISS GROZE. And when that church clock down the street strikes eleven, we shall drink Sir Charles's health round this table.

JIMMY. That was nine o'clock. That is, exactly two hours from now?

MISS GROZE. Good evening.

JIMMY *(stopping her)* Ah! But the important point is, Miss Groze, *why* is Sir Charles giving the party on the stage of the St James's Theatre?

MISS GROZE *(after a pause)* That information is not being granted to the Press.

JIMMY. I say, what fun! Is there some mystery about it?

MISS GROZE. I decline to say anything about anything.

JIMMY *(writing in his notebook)* You are enjoying yourself, aren't you, Miss Groze? I have an inkling, though.

MISS GROZE. An inkling won't help you much.

JIMMY *(still writing)* You never know . . . There was no stage doorkeeper. And there's nobody about . . . Have they run away?

(A pause. He crosses to her. She is very much on the defensive)

Wasn't a little Dago man found—murdered——

(MISS GROZE starts and sinks on the arm of the sofa)

—in a dressing-room in this theatre just over a week ago?

MISS GROZE. Well?

JIMMY. Well, this party's got something to do with it.

MISS GROZE. Has it, indeed?

JIMMY. Yes, it has, indeed.

MISS GROZE. And what has it got to do with it?

JIMMY. That's what *I* want to know.

MISS GROZE. And that's what you'll go on wanting to know.

(MRS WRAGG *comes in from the right of the archway. She has on a long coat and a boa, and a hat clustered with bouquets of artificial flowers. She is looking for somebody*)

That information is not being granted to the Press . . . Are you going out, Wragg?

(*No answer*)

Why are you dressed to go out, Wragg?

MRS WRAGG (*to Jimmy*) 'Ere, young man, you look as if you might be'ave civil to a lady as is one. I'm looking for Sir Charles Jasper. Do you know if Sir Charles is hinside or houtside the theatre at the moment?

JIMMY. I don't know, I'm sure, Mrs Wragg. I'm a stranger in these parts myself.

MISS GROZE. Sir Charles is in his dressing-room. He is resting at the moment, and must not be disturbed.

MRS WRAGG. Young man, is Sir Charles hin or hout?

JIMMY. Sir Charles is in his dressing-room. He is resting at the moment, and must not be disturbed.

MRS WRAGG. Thank you, young man.

JIMMY. It looks as if I'm going to be quite useful to you, Mrs Wragg.

MRS WRAGG. Well, anyway, you don't bite a poor woman's 'ead off like certain people what I know and what I'm not on speaking terms with thank you very much just the same. (*She makes to go*)

MISS GROZE (*rising*) This is beyond a joke, Wragg! You have no business to be going out at this time, when there's nobody to look after things but you and me until after eleven o'clock!

JIMMY. Mrs Wragg, you have no business to be going out at this time, when there's . . .

MRS WRAGG. I know what my business is better than nobody, and I'd have you know, young man, that if you didn't give me my correct title of Mrs, I wouldn't be on no speaking terms with you neither. I'm a cook, not a blinkin' chambermaid!

MISS GROZE (*crossing to her*) Look here, Wragg, this is really going too far!

JIMMY. I should try again. Miss Groze.

MISS GROZE. Look here—Mrs Wragg, really . . .

MRS WRAGG. And I'd have you know, miss, next time you send a nasty fulminating note to me in the basement of this 'ere theatre, that Mrs Wragg is not spelt R.A.G., but W.R.A.G.G.!

MISS GROZE. I object to your making a scene in front of a perfect stranger, who might have the delicacy to know where he's wanted and where he's not!

JIMMY. That's put us both in our places, Mrs Wragg!

MRS WRAGG. It 'as not! An' what's more, I'm not only leavin' this 'ere theatre at the present moment, but I'm leavin' Sir Charles Jasper's service for good and all, and that's what I've come to tell 'im, and that's what I've got me boa'r on for, and me bag downstairs and me impedimenta packed.

JIMMY. But why this sudden flight?

MRS WRAGG (*going up to him, a sudden change in her voice*) Because I'm—frightened.

JIMMY. Frightened?

MRS WRAGG. I'm frightened, that's all, and I'm going.

MISS GROZE (*sitting beside the supper-table*) But you can't go when there's nobody here to look after things but me ...

MRS WRAGG. That's just it! Why isn't there nobody 'ere but you? Tell me that!

MISS GROZE. Because ...

MRS WRAGG. Don't interrupt me when I've got something to get off me mind! Why isn't there nobody 'ere but you? Tell me that! Because everybody else 'as left. An' why 'ave they left? Tell me that! What's become of that 'ousemaid and the two footmen an' the butler what Sir Charles engaged for the party, pro temporairy? Why 'ave they took themselves off this very afternoon as ever was? Tell me that!

MISS GROZE. Because ...

MRS WRAGG. Because they were frightened. There's strange dealings in this 'ere theatre, sir, an' the police ought to know about it.

JIMMY. Do you mean there's a criminal hiding here?

MRS WRAGG. No, not a criminal. You could deal with a criminal. A criminal belongs to this world. These is things that —don't belong to this world ...

JIMMY (*impressed*) Don't belong to this world ... Do you mean—sort of—black magic, and all that?

MISS GROZE. You're letting your imagination run away with you!

MRS WRAGG. I've never let anything nor anybody run away with me! Imagination indeed! Is all them books, all about spiritings and burnings and such like things what everybody's seen with their very own eyes, is them imagination?

MISS GROZE (*making to rise*) Don't make such a fool of yourself.

MRS WRAGG (*pushing* MISS GROZE *down again*) Listen to me! You can talk to me till your head falls off about the march of science and all that, but there's some things beyond the march of science, and always will be. (*Turning back to Jimmy, very quiet and serious again all of a sudden*) My grandfather lived down Dorset way ... 'E knew an old woman what 'ad a string of strange beads round 'er neck, and a idol by 'er bed, and one night, the finest and quietest night of the year, she was found—struck by lightning.

Miss Groze. I still don't see . . .

Mrs Wragg (*a virago again*) That wasn't imagination, was it? An' this isn't neither! Sir Charles, 'e looks 'armless enough, but what with 'is little idols and 'is incantations an' his ghost ideas, I 'ear the police is taking notice, and the asylums as well! An' that's what's driving 'is wife crazy, poor thing!

Jimmy (*with a start*) What's that?

Mrs Wragg. An' 'er still a minor! It's a real crime, it is . . . 'E'll be found one of these days as if there's been lightning about, and 'e won't need no storm neither!

Jimmy. She's worried, is she?

Mrs Wragg. Worried isn't the word!

Miss Groze. You've no proof of anything at all! Anyhow, if you go now, you forfeit your wages . . .

Mrs Wragg. I'm willin' to forfeit anything so long as I get safely out of this 'ere theatre! And proof, my goodness . . .

Miss Groze. Well?

Mrs Wragg (*to Jimmy*) That butler told me a rumour or two. Why 'ave we come 'ere to a blessed empty theatre, tell me that? Why couldn't 'e give 'is party at the Ritz, sir, like you and me? What's all this story of the man who was murdered in the dressing-room?

Miss Groze. Are you suggesting that Sir Charles was the murderer?

Mrs Wragg. Don't you start trying to put me on the wrong track, my lady! There's something very funny about this place. It's in that book. I seen it.

Jimmy. What book?

Mrs Wragg (*pointing to the book on the small table*) That one.

Jimmy (*reading*) "The St James's Theatre Legend, after original manuscripts, by Charles Jasper, the famous authority on the Occult in England."

Mrs Wragg (*taking the book*) Excuse me, there's a very queer bit, sir, on page one hundred and fifteen (*giving him the book*) about a dumb woman. (*Sitting in the armchair*) Fair sent the shivers down my back, it did, specially when you put two and two together! And if you'd seen what I seen just now . . .

Miss Groze (*with a start*) What did you see?

Mrs Wragg. There's a very dark passage outside the wardrobe door.

Miss Groze. Well?

(Jimmy *is reading the book*)

Mrs Wragg. There was somebody walking down it, very slowly, and not making any noise. I couldn't see properly—so I called out—twice . . .

Miss Groze. Go on!

Mrs Wragg. There was no answer.

(*A pause.* Miss Groze *rises in an attempt to control herself, and walks to the foot of the supper-table*)

She just went on walking down the passage . . .

Miss Groze. She?

Mrs Wragg. Yes, I tell you, I'm sure of it! The—dumb woman . . .

(Jimmy *starts, looks up from the book, and looks back again at what he has been reading*)

Mrs Wragg (*rising and making for the door*)   And that's why I'm not staying at this 'ere theatre tonight, not for one 'undred pounds . . .

(Beatrice *comes in from the left of the archway. She is a very pretty girl of twenty, in evening dress.* Jimmy *stands on one side and watches her intently*)

Beatrice. Hallo, Mrs Wragg!

Mrs Wragg (*taken aback*)   Evenin', my lady.

Beatrice. All dressed up to go out?

Mrs Wragg (*still more taken aback*)   Yes, my lady . . .

Beatrice. Something you've forgotten for the party?

Mrs Wragg. No, my lady.

Beatrice. Oh. (*Looking from Miss Groze to Mrs Wragg, her smile fading*)   Has—has anything happened?

Mrs Wragg. No, my lady.

Beatrice (*suddenly afraid*)   Something has happened!

Miss Groze. Really, Lady Jasper, I shouldn't take any notice . . .

Beatrice. Quick, Mrs Wragg! What is it?

Mrs Wragg. Only—that I've seen something upstairs, my lady, and I'm frightened to stay.

Beatrice. You've seen something . . . (*Closing her eyes, and taking Mrs Wragg by the shoulders*)   Mrs Wragg—you—you've been kind to me . . .

Mrs Wragg. And you've been that kind to me too, my lady . . .

Beatrice. Then will you do one thing for me?

Mrs Wragg. Well, my lady . . .

Beatrice. Just one thing!

Mrs Wragg. Yes, I will, my lady.

Beatrice. Will you stay here tonight and keep me company?

Mrs Wragg (*looking out to the back of the stage*)   Stay—here?

Beatrice. Yes. I—I'm rather frightened too . . . I don't know what of, but I am . . . You will stay, won't you?

Mrs Wragg. I—I daren't, my lady.

Beatrice. Oh, please, Mrs Wragg, please!

Mrs Wragg. My lady, I wouldn't stay 'ere tonight, not for a 'undred pounds!

BEATRICE. I thought at least you'd be with me . . . (*Putting her arms round her*) For my sake . . .

MRS WRAGG. My lady, you 've me crestfallen . . . All right, my lady. I'll go and put away me impedimenta and my boa.

(MRS WRAGG *goes out through the door, sheepishly. A pause*)

MISS GROZE. Would you like an aspirin, Lady Jasper?

(BEATRICE *looks at her. There is dislike in her look*)

BEATRICE. No, thank you, Miss Groze. (*Seeing Jimmy*) Oh . . .

MISS GROZE. It's a reporter, Lady Jasper. I'll get rid of him at once . . . (*Crossing to him*) Once and for all, will you . . .

BEATRICE. I'm sorry to drive you away . . .

JIMMY (*looking at her intently*) Not at all, Lady Jasper.

BEATRICE. Oh! (*She starts and looks at him more closely*)

MISS GROZE. I beg your pardon, Lady Jasper?

BEATRICE. Nothing. I merely thought . . .

JIMMY. Thought what?

BEATRICE. I thought for a second you were somebody I'd met before. I'm so sorry.

JIMMY. I wonder if you'd give a struggling journalist a hand?

MISS GROZE. This is the way out, Mr—er——

BEATRICE. And how could I give you a hand?

JIMMY. By giving me, if you would, one or two—(*looking at Miss Groze*) exclusive bits of information.

MISS GROZE. Really . . .

BEATRICE. It's all right, thank you, Miss Groze.

JIMMY. Would you?

(BEATRICE *hesitates*)

(*Crossing to her*) I realize it sounds awful cheek, Lady Jasper.

MISS GROZE. It is!

BEATRICE. Miss Groze, would you mind doing something for me?

MISS GROZE (*with a cold smile*) Certainly, Lady Jasper.

BEATRICE. Would you mind telling the band my husband wants to hear them play, and then—going up to your dressing-room?

MISS GROZE (*her smile fading*) Certainly, Lady Jasper.

(MISS GROZE *goes out to the right of the archway*)

BEATRICE. Well?

JIMMY. Well?

(*He motions* BEATRICE *to the armchair. She sits*)

BEATRICE. Well?

JIMMY. Well?

BEATRICE. You know, somebody's got to say something. (*She is gradually forgetting her distress*)

JIMMY. Then I'll say it. (*Sitting on the sofa*) You recognized me, didn't you?

BEATRICE. I wasn't sure at first. We only met for a second or two . . . But I remember perfectly now! Mr West, at Lady Tawney's tea-party on Tuesday, wasn't it?

JIMMY (*hurt*) Mr North, at Mrs Ackleton's cocktail party on Monday.

BEATRICE. I'm so sorry!

JIMMY. You'd forgotten all about me.

BEATRICE. But, you know, it *was* only a minute . . .

JIMMY. Only a minute—for you.

BEATRICE. I'm afraid you're a very sentimental young man.

JIMMY. Everybody makes fun of me. I don't care.

BEATRICE. And now, suppose we get the interview over!

JIMMY. I'm—not a reporter at all!

BEATRICE. Not a reporter at all?

JIMMY. Not a reporter at all! (*With a laugh*) Never set foot in a newspaper office in my life!

(BEATRICE *finds his laugh infectious*)

BEATRICE. I thought perhaps you hadn't.

JIMMY. Oh?

BEATRICE. You carried a notebook. So you're untruthful as well as sentimental?

JIMMY. It's in a good cause!

BEATRICE. What?

JIMMY (*rising*) You.

(BEATRICE *is obviously amused.* JIMMY *stands first on one foot, then on the other. He sits, to find he has sat on his hat. He rises again*)

Am I being ridiculous?

BEATRICE. A little.

JIMMY. Oh.

BEATRICE. But quite amusing.

JIMMY. Miss Groze didn't think so.

BEATRICE (*depressed again*) Oh, that woman . . .

JIMMY. Don't you like her either?

BEATRICE. No.

JIMMY. I'm so glad! Looks as if she'd been christened with vinegar and never recovered!

BEATRICE (*joining in his laugh*) I never thought of that. . . . (*Suddenly stern*) You know, Mr North, I'm prepared to allow that it's romantic to visit ladies under an assumed name, but, you know, it might be misinterpreted.

JIMMY. I'm afraid you're going to disapprove of me.

BEATRICE. I don't disapprove of you.

JIMMY. You don't? Oh—(*sitting*) you don't know how marvellous it feels to be approved of by you!

BEATRICE. It doesn't mean I approve of you either, particularly.

JIMMY. Oh. It merely means you don't take me seriously enough to do either?

BEATRICE. Probably.

JIMMY (*rising with a sigh*) I thought so.

BEATRICE. Well, why was I going to disapprove of you?

JIMMY. Because, as well as being a liar, I'm an eavesdropper!

BEATRICE. You didn't mean to say you listen at keyholes?

JIMMY. I listened while your husband was helping you on with your things after that party.

BEATRICE. Oh? I don't remember . . .

JIMMY. I do. He said, "By the way, darling"—(*brandishing the telephone receiver*) how I loathed him when he said that! (*Putting back the receiver*) Oh, I'm so sorry . . .

BEATRICE. And what did he say then?

JIMMY. He said, "By the way, darling, I've written to the theatre people."

BEATRICE. The theatre people?

JIMMY. "And they rang up and said we could take possession of the theatre as soon as we liked."

BEATRICE (*her gaiety gone*) Oh . . .

JIMMY. You remember now? And you turned to him, looking terribly worried, and you said, "Charles, I know it's playing with fire! Give your party anywhere else but there!"

BEATRICE. Yes . . .

JIMMY. And all he said was "Nonsense!" And you said, "I'm terrified of it, Charles, I'm terrified!" And you looked it.

BEATRICE. Well?

JIMMY (*sitting on the sofa*) Ever since that night your look of terror has worried me. I knew there was something seriously the matter. And I had to come here, tonight, under an assumed name, as a reporter . . .

BEATRICE (*curiously*) Why did you come under an assumed name as a reporter?

JIMMY. Why, to help you, in case . . .

BEATRICE. I know. But you could have come here under your own name and as your own self, perfectly easily, and asked me if I needed rescuing!

JIMMY (*taken aback*) Could I? I suppose I could . . . Anyway, it was damn cheek.

BEATRICE (*after consideration*) It was rather sporting . . . Thank you very much.

(*She rises and walks to the archway, as if to give him his congé. He goes up to her, reluctantly*)

JIMMY. Just now, when Mrs Wragg said she was leaving, you can't deny you were frightened.

BEATRICE (*with an effort*) I wasn't feeling myself. I'm all right now. Honestly. Good-bye, Mr North . . .

(MISS GROZE *rushes in between them, from the right, and collapses at the supper-table with a stifled cry. They stand over her in consternation*)

JIMMY. What on earth's the matter?

BEATRICE. Some water, quick . . .

MISS GROZE. No—no . . . It's all right . . .

BEATRICE. What is it? (*Her voice trembling*) Quick! What have you seen?

MISS GROZE. I'll be all right—in a minute . . . I was just turning the corner of the stairs, and just going to turn on the light. It looked like—well, like she said—a—something—moving . . .

BEATRICE (*dully*) The—dumb woman . . . You saw her?

JIMMY. Of course she didn't!

BEATRICE. And Mrs Wragg saw her too . . .

JIMMY. Nonsense!

MISS GROZE (*glaring up at him*) It's not nonsense! (*Collecting herself with an effort*)) I'm all right now . . . It was the dark.

BEATRICE. I—I expect that was it, Miss Groze. Don't you think you'd better go and lie down for a minute or two?

MISS GROZE. Yes. (*Rising and going to the right opening*) Thank you, Lady Jasper . . . I'm afraid I've been silly.

(MISS GROZE *goes out through the right opening. A moment's silence.* BEATRICE *crosses and sits on the sofa*)

JIMMY. Well, we'd better go on where we were interrupted.

BEATRICE (*mechanically*) Yes.

JIMMY. Which means I go on saying good-bye and go.

BEATRICE (*her face averted*) Yes.

JIMMY (*expectantly*) Good-bye.

BEATRICE. Good-bye.

JIMMY (*disappointed*) Good-bye. (*He walks slowly to the archway*)

BEATRICE (*suddenly*) No, no!

JIMMY (*running eagerly down to the back of the sofa*) Well?

BEATRICE. Don't go . . .

JIMMY. Yes?

BEATRICE. Don't—go . . .

JIMMY. What—what's the matter?

BEATRICE (*clasping his arm, almost in sobs*) Don't go—don't go —don't go . . .

JIMMY. No jolly fear! (*Climbing over the edge of the sofa to her side*) I'm staying!

(*He laughs, and in spite of herself she laughs too, her head almost on his shoulder. She recovers gradually*)

JIMMY. There! You do feel better, don't you? Yes? Yes!
BEATRICE. Yes—I feel better . . .
JIMMY. And I feel fine.
BEATRICE. I'm sorry I made a scene.
JIMMY. I can see there's something seriously wrong with this place.

(MRS ARTHUR *comes in from the right of the archway. She is a handsome sharp-faced woman of forty-five, dressed in a smart but rather loud evening frock. She is not quite well-bred, and a born bully. She carries two low bowls of flowers; she arranges them on the supper-table, and cuts the flowers with a pair of scissors which she has brought in with her*)

Now what I want to know is this. What has the fact of Sir Charles giving his party on the stage of the St James's Theatre, London, got to do with this legend of the St James's Theatre I hear so much about?
MRS ARTHUR. I'm sick and tired of the legend of the St James's Theatre, so please, whoever you are, don't mention it in my presence again tonight . . . (*Staring at them, and then over the theatre*) Are you—rehearsing for something?
JIMMY (*rising*) Oh . . .
BEATRICE. Mr North, my mother.
MRS ARTHUR (*brandishing the scissors at him*) How do you do?
JIMMY. How do you do?
MRS ARTHUR (*suddenly*) Weren't you the young man at the cocktail party I went to with my daughter?

(JIMMY *is obviously reminded of a distressing episode and moves down to the left of the sofa*)

JIMMY. Oh, yes . . .
MRS ARTHUR. You were very drunk.
JIMMY. I had three cocktails!
MRS ARTHUR. You were very drunk.
JIMMY. I had three cocktails!
MRS ARTHUR (*implacably*) You were very drunk.
JIMMY. I had three c—— (*Sitting hopelessly on the pouffe*) Yes.
MRS ARTHUR. *And* you were very rude to me about my dress.
JIMMY (*brightly*) Oh, yes! Something about lace curtains, I . . . Oh, I beg your pardon.
MRS ARTHUR (*freezingly*) Granted. (*Cutting her flowers again*) And what are you doing here, frightening my daughter about this perfectly ridiculous St James's Theatre legend?
JIMMY. It seems to me, Mrs Arthur, that your daughter doesn't need frightening.
MRS ARTHUR. I'm a rather better judge of what my daughter needs, thank you! *And* of what she does not need.
BEATRICE. Mother!

Mrs Arthur. I'm sorry, Beatrice, but I find great difficulty in disguising from you the fact that I definitely dislike this young man.

Jimmy (*incredulously*) You don't!

Mrs Arthur. I do. So nice of you to have called.

Jimmy. Oh, do you think so?

(Mrs Arthur *holds out her hand in dismissal. He rises as if to go.* Beatrice *gives him a look of entreaty*)

I—I'm afraid Lady Jasper has invited me to stay on.

Mrs Arthur. To stay on? But, Beatrice, until half-past eleven it's practically a family party!

Beatrice. I don't think Charles will mind, Mother.

(Jimmy *takes off his overcoat with a triumphant smile*)

Mrs Arthur. Well!

Beatrice. Mother, I'm frightened!

Mrs Arthur (*sitting in the armchair; impatiently*) Oh, fiddle-sticks!

Beatrice. You're frightened too.

Mrs Arthur (*starting*) I?

Beatrice. You're all on edge, Mother!

Mrs Arthur (*taking up a cigarette*) Do you really think I'm such a blithering idiot as to get nervy because there's a stupid rigmarole about this theatre being haunted . . .

(*She strikes a match on the last word. Silence. The match flares in an otherwise motionless scene. They all seem to be listening*)

Beatrice. Haunted . . .

Mrs Arthur. I—I thought I heard somebody moving out there . . . How—how quiet it is . . . (*Pulling herself together angrily and blowing out the match*) Oh, what nonsense . . . (*She rises*) It's that silly book! (*She takes it off the back of the sofa and crosses to the door with it*) I don't care what Charles says, I'm going to throw it out of my dressing-room window.

(Sir Charles Jasper *appears from the right of the archway. He is a mild professorial gentleman with grey hair, looks nearer fifty than forty, and wears a dinner jacket with a white carnation in the button-hole.* Mrs Arthur *is taken aback and sits at the head of the supper-table*)

Jasper (*looking round him*) I say! Isn't that splendid? Exactly like a real play! (*Kissing Beatrice absently on the forehead*) How are you, darling?

Beatrice (*a little diffidently*) Charles, this is Mr North, a friend of mine. I've asked him to join us at supper.

Jasper (*absently*) Oh, really? Good . . . I say, Beatrice, wasn't that a perfectly splendid idea of mine, to have the curtain raised, and all the lights on, exactly like a real play! (*Moving round the stage*) I say, we *are* going to have the most original party that was ever thought of! And marvellous for my little experiment! (*To Mrs Arthur*) What are you going to do with my book?

MRS ARTHUR. I—I . . .

JIMMY. She's going to throw it out of her dressing-room window!

JASPER (*suddenly angry and authoritative*)   Give it to me!

MRS ARTHUR (*obeying meekly*)   I'm so sorry, Charles . . .

JASPER (*sternly*)   This book is the study of a lifetime.

JIMMY (*moving up to him*)   But what *is* your little experiment, sir? I'm longing to know, and nobody will tell me. Won't you, sir? Please do!

JASPER.   Tonight is my great night, and that not only because I inherit two million pounds, young man! Tonight, I'm going to see proved, on this very spot, the legend of the St James's Theatre!

JIMMY.   Well, sir, won't you sit down and tell me all about it?

JASPER.   Well . . . (*Sitting in the armchair*) It's not a long story, but rather a wonderful, and rather a horrible one.

JIMMY.   Yes, sir? (*Sitting on the edge of the sofa*) Go on!

JASPER (*impressively, his mild ineffectiveness gone*)   One morning, ninety-five years ago, on the stage of this theatre, an old man was found—murdered.

JIMMY.   Yes?

JASPER.   He was identified as Robert Battersby, a notorious alchemist, and a practiser of black magic.

JIMMY.   Black magic . . . Yes?

JASPER.   He was dumb.

JIMMY.   Oh . . .

JASPER.   He had supernatural powers which were extraordinary, and—(*holding up his book*) have been proved over and over again . . . Among his papers they found a document that swore, on all sorts of terrible strange oaths . . .

JIMMY.   Yes?

JASPER.   It swore that if ever he were murdered, within ten days of his death, on the spot where the murder had taken place —(*putting the book down on the little table*) his ghost would walk.

(*A pause. Even* JIMMY *is awed*)

JIMMY.   Sounds pretty gruesome.

JASPER.   There's a still more gruesome part to come . . .

JIMMY.   Go on, sir!

JASPER.   He said that the advent of the ghost would be heralded in a certain way.

JIMMY.   How?

JASPER.   He said a woman would be found, wandering round the place of the murder, and that she would be dumb.

JIMMY.   Because he had been dumb!

JASPER. He said that the moment when the woman recovered her speech would be the moment when the ghost was near, but before it could be seen——
BEATRICE. Oh, Charles, it's too horrible!
JASPER. —before the ghost could be seen, the woman would have to suffer violent death at its hands.
JIMMY. And what happened?
JASPER. For ten days a close watch was kept all around this theatre . . . About the fifth day a little old gipsy woman was found walking by the river. She spoke by signs . . . On the eighth day she suddenly recovered her speech . . . They found out she was a sort of medium—what they called a witch. (*Rising*) They let her go . . . Three hours later her body was found——
JIMMY. Her body!
JASPER. —on the stage of this theatre.
JIMMY (*in a whisper*) Say . . .
JASPER. And on the ninth day, it was witnessed by fifteen people that the ghost of the murdered man walked down the stage of this theatre.

(BEATRICE *controls herself with an effort*)

JIMMY. Please, Lady Jasper, don't upset yourself . . .
BEATRICE. I—I'm all right, really. . . .
JIMMY. But, sir, I don't see what all that has got to do with your giving the party here . . .
JASPER. Ah! (*Sitting* L) There was another thing in Battersby's document. He swore that if anyone else were murdered on the site of his own murder, another strange woman would be found —and the ghost of the murdered man would walk.
JIMMY. Well?
JASPER. Last week, just after I had practically decided to give tonight's party at the Berkeley, I read in the paper that a strange man had just been shot dead, in the St James's Theatre.
JIMMY. Ah! I see . . . I—see.
JASPER. Ever since I have had people watching the place night and day. There has been no sign of anything unusual. Tonight is the tenth night since the murder.
JIMMY. And Battersby gave ten nights as the time limit?
JASPER. Yes.
BEATRICE. And Mrs Wragg saw a woman in one of those passages . . .
JASPER. What!
MRS ARTHUR. Or thinks she did! Hysterical nonsense . . .
BEATRICE. Miss Groze did too!
JASPER. Miss Groze!

(*He is obviously as delighted as* MRS ARTHUR *is taken aback*)

BEATRICE. I spent the afternoon reading that book. It's terrible,

like being in the Middle Ages again, living in dark corners of the
mind that nobody knows about . . . incantations—curses—sym-
bols—images of burnt wood . . .

JASPER (*lost to them all*) Tonight a ghost is going to cross the
stage of this theatre . . .

BEATRICE. I must have somebody I can trust to . . . (*Clasping
Jimmy's arm, suddenly*) Don't go! Please don't go!

MRS ARTHUR. Beatrice! (*She rises*)

JASPER. Now, now! I'm sorry if I frightened you, my dear.
Now forget about it!

MRS ARTHUR (*crossing to Beatrice and sitting beside her on the sofa*)
What is much more important, dear, is that at eleven o'clock
tonight your husband inherits two million pounds, and you ought
to be proud of him!

JASPER (*with a chuckle*) Two million! To the eternal discom-
fiture of my distant relative and rival Maurice Mullins!

(JIMMY *offers Mrs Arthur a cigarette*)

That is, unless Mr Maurice Mullins has the impertinence to do
away with me before eleven o'clock!

MRS ARTHUR (*looking up from the cigarette-case to its owner, with a
start*) Maurice Mullins. . . .

JASPER (*rising and going up towards the archway*) Well, suppose we
give my little jazz band a chance to be heard, and then change . . .

MRS ARTHUR (*rising and going swiftly to him*) One moment,
Charles!

JASPER. Yes?

MRS ARTHUR. Before we go up, I'd like to put one or two
questions to—(*suddenly turning on Jimmy*) this young man!

JIMMY (*surprised*) Oh yes?

MRS ARTHUR. Why did you choose such a very odd hour to
visit my daughter, and tonight of all nights?

JASPER. My dear . . .

MRS ARTHUR. Well?

JIMMY (*at sea*) I wasn't—I didn't—I hadn't—I wasn't visiting
her the way you mean at all—and I came to see if I could be of
any help . . .

MRS ARTHUR. Charles, call your secretary!

JASPER. But . . .

MRS ARTHUR. Call your secretary, I tell you!

JASPER. But . . .

MRS ARTHUR. I'm doing this for your own personal protec-
tion, so will you please call your secretary!

(JASPER *is about to go when* MISS GROZE *opens the door*)

JASPER. Oh, there you are, Miss Groze. Now.

MRS ARTHUR. Miss Groze, have you ever seen this person
before?

MISS GROZE. Who? . . . Oh, yes, Mrs Arthur. Half an hour ago. He's a reporter.

MRS ARTHUR. A reporter? Ah! . . . His name?

MISS GROZE. He doesn't know, he's not sure if it's Simon Richardson or Richard Symonson.

MRS ARTHUR (*all her suspicions confirmed*) Ah! It may interest you to know, Miss Groze, that he has now added a third to his collection. That of Mr North . . . (*Producing the revolver from the drawer of the small table*) Hands up!

(JIMMY *is dumbfounded, but his hands shoot up automatically*)

JASPER. Are you mad?

MRS ARTHUR. Don't you dare move!

JIMMY. Not on your life!

BEATRICE. Mother, it'll go off in a minute and then where will you be?

JIMMY. What is more to the point, where will *I* be?

MRS ARTHUR. Well, young man, may I add still another name to your collection?

JIMMY. Do.

MRS ARTHUR. The name of Sir Charles Jasper's only living relative, Mr Maurice Mullins!

JASPER. What!

JIMMY (*making to sit*) Not guilty, thank you very much!

MRS ARTHUR. Get up! I'm rather glad now I smuggled this revolver in here. Something has been telling me all day you'd turn up before eleven o'clock tonight. I advise you to be a little less clumsy next time you try and snatch a fortune at the last minute . . . Charles, telephone the police!

BEATRICE. Mother, are you mad?

MRS ARTHUR. Do you realize, Charles, that this man has in-sinuated himself in here with the intention of murdering you before eleven o'clock to-night?

JIMMY. Have—have I?

MRS ARTHUR. I would hardly call you the perfect criminal, Mr Mullins! You have every appearance of guilt!

JIMMY. Have—have I?

MRS ARTHUR. Charles, will you or will you not telephone the police?

(JASPER *decides to humour her and stoops under the revolver to take up the telephone*)

JIMMY. Half a second, sir, please! Lady Jasper, would you dive into my breast pocket and fish out my case?

(BEATRICE *obeys*)

MRS ARTHUR (*apprehensive*) What is it, Beatrice?

BEATRICE (*dryly*) The passport of a Mr James North

MRS ARTHUR (*dropping the revolver slowly, more mortified than relieved*) Oh . . .

(MRS WRAGG *enters from the right opening, sees the revolver, gives a gasp, and goes out again.* MR CAVENDISH *and his band get into their places in the orchestra pit.*
MISS GROZE *goes out to the right of the archway*)

JASPER. I appreciate your solicitude, my dear, but you must realize one thing . . . If the said Maurice Mullins were a criminal, he would never dare come here today, under the most impenetrable of disguises, with the intention of—(*taking the revolver from her and putting it back in the drawer*) of murdering me.

(MRS ARTHUR *sits sheepishly in the armchair*)

What with the terms of the will and everything, the evidence would be too damning . . . Well, that's that. Phew!

(MRS WRAGG *comes in again*)

MRS WRAGG. Excuse me, sir.
JASPER. Yes, Mrs Wragg?
MRS WRAGG (*with a gulp*) About the curtain, sir.
JASPER. What's the matter, Mrs Wragg?
MRS WRAGG. Feeling a bit nervy, sir . . . About the curtain, sir, the safety curtain, sir—you said . . .
JASPER. Oh, yes! I got a little reminder from the London County Council this afternoon, to say that our little adventure is equivalent to a stage performance, and the safety curtain must be lowered once. Do that now, before we forget, will you?
MRS WRAGG (*going*) Yes, sir.
JASPER. Do you know how to work the lever, or whatever it is?
MRS WRAGG. Yes, sir, the men showed me before they left this morning. You see, sir, it's quite 'ydraulic. Though as work for one weak woman it is irksome in the extreme.

(MRS WRAGG *goes out through the right opening*)

JASPER. Well, you don't look as if you were off to a wedding, any of you! Are you ready, gentlemen?
CAVENDISH. Yes, sir . . .

(MISS GROZE *rushes in from the right of the archway*)

MISS GROZE. She—she's there again! The woman! The woman we're waiting for! Somebody's coming downstairs . . . She's coming downstairs!

(*She runs to a corner of the stage. They follow suit, looking, fascinated, at the archway. A pause.*
A bland and charming young MAN *comes in from the right of the archway and stands on the threshold. He is in full evening dress, with*

top-hat and stick, and smokes a cigarette. He comes slowly down, smiling)

THE MAN. How do you do? . . . I hope you don't object to my smoking? *(Flicking the ash off his cigarette with a delightful smile)* My name's Maurice Mullins.

MRS WRAGG *(in the wings)* Mind yourselves! The curtain's comin' down!

The band strikes up a lively fox-trot, and the SAFETY CURTAIN comes down.

It is about 9.20, and there is now——

AN INTERVAL

of ten minutes, during which CAVENDISH rehearses his band for the party. Just on half-past nine, the last tune is brought to a sweeping finish.

MR CAVENDISH and his band go under the stage, and the SAFETY CURTAIN rises slowly on——

ACT II

The supper-table is now set for six. MAURICE MULLINS *is sitting in the armchair, the centre of a group.* BEATRICE *and* MRS ARTHUR *are sitting on the sofa;* MISS GROZE *stands near the archway,* JASPER *behind the sofa; and* JIMMY *stands distrustful guard behind Mullins' chair. Social chatter.*

JASPER (*as the Curtain goes slowly up*) Oh, no—it's a hydraulic curtain, she could never work it by herself . . .
MRS WRAGG (*in the wings*) Curtain's up, sir!
JASPER. Thank you, Mrs Wragg. (*To Mullins*) There you are!
MULLINS. A real theatre! Lights all on, scenery, everything! When I was interpreter to the British Embassy in Afghanistan, I noticed—none of the natives ate coco-nuts.

(*The clock strikes half-past nine. They look at him, not knowing what to make of it*)

BEATRICE. Another cocktail?
MULLINS. Well, that's uncommonly kind of you, Lady Jasper . . .

(MISS GROZE *goes out through the door*)

I remember in Afghanistan, playing in the Amateur Dramatic Society's production of the *Mikado*—I was playing the title rôle—you must often have played in amateur theatricals, Mrs—er——
MRS ARTHUR. Arthur.
MULLINS. Mrs Arthur, yes. They tell me they're very fashionable in Society over here.

(*This would have thoroughly charmed* MRS ARTHUR *if she were not thoroughly charmed already*)

JASPER. I—er—saw you put several photographs into your overcoat before you hung it behind that door. It would be a great privilege to see pictures of you—er—depicting various rôles.
MULLINS (*almost to himself*) Depicting various rôles—ha! Certainly, I have several . . . Excuse me.

(MULLINS *goes out through the door. They look at one another in silence*)

JASPER. Well?
MRS ARTHUR. Charming.
JASPER. Well, young man?
JIMMY. I think he's a bore.
JASPER. Well, Beatrice?

24

BEATRICE. He seems very sociable.

JASPER. Oh. Why don't you like him?

BEATRICE. Well, it isn't exactly that. But . . .

JASPER. The real point, of course, lies not so much in what he is, but *who* he is!

JIMMY. Well, I thought he said he was Maurice Mullins . . .

MRS ARTHUR. But he can't be Maurice Mullins! If Maurice Mullins wanted to come here tonight, he would at least have the sense to use an assumed name . . .

JIMMY. Such as James North.

(MULLINS *comes back with several snapshots*)

MULLINS (*sitting in the armchair*) Now let me see—here's one of the polo team resting outside the canteen . . . (*Handing it over to Mrs Arthur*) Those are the team in the foreground, what you see in the background are mountains . . . The one marked with a cross is me. No, the man, not the mountain. Isn't it jolly?

MRS ARTHUR. Yes, sweet . . .

JASPER (*edging round*) I—I do apologize sincerely for my rudeness but I—er—we none of us quite caught your name when you came in . . .

MULLINS. But didn't you get my letter? . . . Oh, I forgot to post it, how silly of me! I arrived home from the East three days ago, and read in the papers about the windfall descending on you tonight, Sir Charles, and about the wonderful party you are giving. I wrote to congratulate you, and now reinforce my congratulations in person! My name is Maurice Mullins.

(*They start. A pause. He looks unconcernedly at his snapshots*)

Maurice Austin Mullins. Austin (*to Jimmy*) to my friends. Profession, journalist, struggling. I'm afraid my sole claim to fame is that I'm supposed to be your only living relative . . . Let me see, what's this one of?

(*The others exchange mixed glances over his head*)

I think it's the palm avenue at Bombay . . . No, no, it's the Dramatic Society dinner, so sorry. The one with the cross is me. No, no, that's a waiter—this one's me . . .

(MRS ARTHUR *decides it is futile to suspect such a very delightful young man*)

JASPER. Well—I had no idea . . .

MULLINS. Neither had I, until I saw in the paper that by your most tactless survival, Sir Charles, I am to be defrauded of two million pounds, of which I stand sorely in need!

JASPER (*tapping Mrs Arthur playfully on the shoulder*) It may interest you to know, Mr Mullins, that you have tonight been suspected of introducing yourself into this theatre under an assumed name, with a view to murdering me before eleven and collaring my fortune!

MULLINS (*with a laugh*) Sir Charles, I only wish I had the brains or the pluck to do it.

JASPER. Well, we're delighted to meet you, Mr Mullins.

MULLINS. I'm delighted too. (*Rising*) And now I must be going.

MRS ARTHUR. Oh, no!

(MISS GROZE *appears at the door with a cocktail*)

Do have your cocktail, anyway!

MULLINS (*taking it*) Oh, thank you.

JASPER. Let you go when you're my only living relative turned up out of the blue? You stay.

(MISS GROZE *crosses behind the sofa*)

MULLINS (*drinking*) But, you see, I have to pay the penalties of being even a struggling journalist. I have a short story I've simply got to get off to the City before midnight . . .

JASPER. Got it with you?

MULLINS (*putting down his glass on the supper-table*) Eh—yes.

JASPER. You can finish it here!

MULLINS. Marvellous! (*Going to the door*) I'll go and fetch it. Oh—I'm afraid I can't possibly stay after all.

JASPER. Why not this time?

MULLINS. My wife's waiting up for me.

JASPER (*taking the receiver off the telephone*) What's the number?

MULLINS. Kensington nine-one-two-seven.

JASPER (*into the telephone*) Kensington nine-one-two-seven. (*Giving him the instrument*) I always have my own way, sir! Please tell her you are out for the evening.

MULLINS. Well, if you insist. I say, how does this telephone manage to work?

JASPER. I had an extension put in from the stage door yesterday.

MULLINS. Oh . . . That you, Bettikins, darling? Yes, this is Toto . . . Listen, Bettikins darling . . . I've just been asked to rather a wonderful party . . . Please, darling . . . No, darling, I promise . . . Only two glasses . . . Good night, darling, love and kisses . . . (*Hanging up*) Sweet little woman . . . Excuse me while I fetch my manuscript, will you?

(*He nearly collides with* JIMMY *on his way to the door*)

Hallo!

(MULLINS *goes out through the door*)

JIMMY. Well, either he's just back from his honeymoon, or Bettikins darling is a very wonderful woman!

JASPER. Pleasant, but not intelligent. I think my fortune's safe while he's about . . . What do you say, Miss Groze?

MISS GROZE. A harmless man, Sir Charles.

MRS ARTHUR. He wouldn't hurt a fly!

JASPER. Silence from the other two! Well?

BEATRICE. I don't know what to think.

JIMMY (*rather ominously*) Neither do I.

(MULLINS *returns with his manuscript*)

MULLINS (*nearly colliding with* JIMMY *again*) Hallo! Work before play, Sir Charles! (*Crossing to the small table and taking up* Jasper's *book*) Oh! So you're an author, too?

JASPER (*flattered*) Well . . .

(MULLINS *crosses to the supper-table and sits, using the book as a rest for his manuscript.* JASPER *is taken aback*)

MULLINS. Oh, Sir Charles, I wonder if I might ask your secretary to help me with these papers?

MRS ARTHUR. I'm sure Miss Groze wouldn't mind.

MISS GROZE. Certainly, Mr Mullins, I'm free at the moment. (*She crosses to the head of the supper-table*)

MULLINS. That's awfully good of you, Miss—er——

MISS GROZE. Groze.

MULLINS. Thank you . . . It would merely consist in blotting each of these pages as I number it.

MISS GROZE (*putting on horn-rimmed spectacles*) Certainly, Mr Mullins.

MULLINS (*putting on horn-rimmed spectacles*) Thank you so much . . . Two . . . Three . . .

JASPER. Oh, Mr Mullins, before we go any further, I feel I ought to tell you that you're in for a most exciting evening . . .

MULLINS. Oh, really?

JASPER. There's been a murder in this theatre . . .

MULLINS. A murder? How thrilling!

JASPER. And there will be a ghost, Mr Mullins . . .

(*The telephone rings. They are startled*)

Oh, bother it . . . Answer it, will you, Miss Groze?

MISS GROZE (*taking off the receiver*) Yes?

BEATRICE. I gave orders nobody was to ring up from the house . . .

MRS ARTHUR. Then who . . .?

MISS GROZE. Sir Charles, it's Johnson.

JASPER (*interested at once*) Johnson, eh?

BEATRICE. Then it's something important . . .

MULLINS. I say, Sir Charles, am I in the way?

JASPER. No, no . . .

MISS GROZE. He's got a message for you, Sir Charles, from the police.

(MULLINS *looks up*)

Shall I repeat it?

JASPER. Yes, yes . . .

MISS GROZE. The police have rung up to tell him that—(*repeating*) "A young Italian has confessed to the so-called St James's Theatre murder of last week."

JASPER. Good . . .

(MULLINS *goes on with his writing*)

MISS GROZE. "He also confesses that—though the body was discovered *in* the St James's Theatre, the actual murder was committed in King Street, and the body dragged into the St James's Theatre during the absence of the night watchman." . . . Goodbye, Johnson.

(*She hangs up, and goes back to the head of the supper-table. They are all immeasurably relieved, except* JASPER, *who sits in the armchair, the picture of disillusionment*)

MRS ARTHUR. So there hasn't been a murder in this theatre at all!

JIMMY. There you are, Lady Jasper! And there's nothing to fear!

BEATRICE. Thank God!

MRS ARTHUR. And all that nonsense about seeing a dumb woman! It just shows you what reading those silly books can do to you . . . And there'll be no ghost! How can there be a ghost, if there's no murder?

MULLINS. Don't be too optimistic . . . (*He rises*)

(*They stare at him*)

Oh, just one of my jokes . . . But this message isn't going to make you give up your delightfully original party, is it?

JASPER. No. But I'm afraid I've lost all interest in the whole thing.

BEATRICE (*happy again*) Well, I suggest we break up for the moment, and go and change into our costumes!

(*She rises and goes to the back of the sofa.* MRS ARTHUR *rises and crosses to Mullins*)

MRS ARTHUR. Mr Mullins, you'll find plenty of choice in the wardrobe! All change now, into the costumes of the Ghosts of History, and on with the candle-light and champagne!

MULLINS. I adore champagne!

MRS ARTHUR. Beatrice, what did it need but Charles's long-lost relative to make the party complete?

BEATRICE (*after a pause, her dislike evident*) It needed—only that.
MRS ARTHUR. Beatrice!
MULLINS (*returning Beatrice's look*) I'm glad you think so, Lady Jasper.
JASPER (*rising and making to go up to the archway*) Ah, well . . . Hallo!

(*He is staring into the alcove. They look*)

What . . . (*He goes up to the alcove and stares at the empty armchair in it*)

(*A pause. JIMMY makes to pass him into the alcove*)

Don't go in there! You'll disturb him.

(*A pause*)

JIMMY. Disturb—him?
JASPER. That man—lying in that chair.

(*A pause*)

BEATRICE. But—but what does he look like?
JASPER. Can't you see? Wearing a dinner-jacket, and a white carnation?
MULLINS. But there's nothing there . . . (*Crossing to the alcove and sitting in the chair, smiling*) Look!
JASPER (*with a start*) But you're sitting—just where I saw him!
BEATRICE. And you don't see him now?
JASPER. N-no. Not now. How very odd!
MULLINS (*rising, coming down with his papers and sitting on the sofa*) How very odd, Sir Charles, that you should be wearing a dinner-jacket and a white carnation.

(*JASPER looks at his buttonhole. A pause, full of foreboding*)

MRS ARTHUR. Oh, but—but it's quite natural—so many men might!
JASPER. Of course . . . (*He closes the curtains abruptly over the alcove*) Well, I'm going to change . . . See you soon!

(*JASPER goes out to the right of the archway, a little constrained and shaken. They are all nervous, except MULLINS. A pause*)

MULLINS. What an extraordinary thing! Anybody would think the theatre really was haunted.
BEATRICE. I—I suppose we'd better get changed too . . .
MRS ARTHUR. Beatrice, you might at least say one word of welcome to your new guest!
BEATRICE (*with forced pleasantness, to Mullins*) I hope you'll enjoy yourself . . .
MULLINS. Thank you, Lady Jasper . . . Lady Jasper, I'm sorry you don't like me.

MRS ARTHUR. Beatrice! Why don't you like Mr Mullins?

BEATRICE. I—I don't know . . .

MULLINS. Oh, Lady Jasper!

BEATRICE (*collecting herself*) I'm so sorry . . .

(*She makes to follow* JIMMY *to the right of the archway*)

MULLINS. So am I . . . Five . . . Six . . .

MRS ARTHUR. Are you two going up together?

JIMMY. Yes.

MRS ARTHUR. I'll come with you.

JIMMY. Certainly . . . Oh—you go on up. I'll follow in a second.

(*He turns back and stares intently at Mullins.* MISS GROZE *crosses to them.*

    BEATRICE *and* MRS ARTHUR *go out through the archway*)

MULLINS (*looking up with a wide smile*) Hallo! (*Holding up his papers*) No, it's not very good. . . .

(JIMMY *looks from one to the other, gives it up, and follows the others.* MISS GROZE *sits beside Mullins on the sofa*)

Let me see . . . How far had I numbered? . . . Seven, eight, nine, ten . . .

(*A pause. They look at each other, and both at the same time take off their spectacles*)

MISS GROZE. I was interested in the telephone conversation with your wife.

MULLINS. Interested enough to notice I had my finger on the hook all the time? . . . Eleven.

MISS GROZE (*amused*) No, I didn't notice.

MULLINS. I don't talk like that to my wife. Twelve.

MISS GROZE. And you're married.

MULLINS. What? (*With a sigh*) Thirteen.

MISS GROZE. Officially married?

MULLINS. Yes.

MISS GROZE. Why?

MULLINS. Her mother. I used to call her mother Rod of Iron.

MISS GROZE. What was the attraction?

MULLINS. She told me she had money. She betrayed me.

MISS GROZE. Ran off with another man?

MULLINS. No, she had no money. Fourteen, fifteen . . .

MISS GROZE. What's her name? What does she look like?

MULLINS. Sixteen, seventeen . . . Elizabeth. She's at the flat. She's sweet . . . You haven't changed a bit, my dear. Not a day older. Elizabeth's at the flat. Not well. A headache. Poor thing. Eighteen.

MISS GROZE. And you still write, the same as you did when I married . . .

MULLINS. You, married? My dear, I never heard this before!

MISS GROZE. Oh, yes, I married.

MULLINS. My dear!

MISS GROZE. I married you.

MULLINS. Oh, yes, of course. Twenty, twenty-one.

MISS GROZE. Not officially, though. I had no Rod of Iron . . . I used to provide the love interest for your stories. Who provides it now?

MULLINS. I don't write love stories any more. I write about the problems of married life. Pays better, and comes easier to me. Twenty-two, twenty-three.

MISS GROZE. Well?

MULLINS. Tell me more, my dear.

MISS GROZE. I applied for the post as soon as I got your letter.

MULLINS. And there really is a will, mentioning me as the next heir?

MISS GROZE. I saw it this morning. That's why I sent you that telegram.

MULLINS. And only just in time too! By Jove! I gambled on a rumour, and I won!

MISS GROZE (*curious and amused*) Austin, what—what are you hoping to do?

MULLINS (*putting his papers down on the floor*) Look here, my dear, you're one of the most sensible women I've ever met. Use your sense now. What do you think I'm hoping to do? Drink a glass of champagne and go home to my little Bettikins? (*Looking into her eyes*) Is there a doctor near the theatre?

(*A pause. Her smile fades. She draws back, a terrible suspicion dawning on her*)

MISS GROZE. Austin! You—you don't mean . . .!

MULLINS. Of course I do!

MISS GROZE. You do! (*Staring at him*) I never dreamt you meant that. (*Suddenly hysterical*) I won't go on! I won't! I won't!

(*He has her by the wrists*)

MULLINS. Be quiet and listen to me! (*He rises and surveys the theatre coolly*) There's something about a theatre that always makes me want to make a speech. (*He advances to the footlights and looks out into the darkness of the auditorium*)

MISS GROZE. Austin—please!

MULLINS. I've studied myself for years, and I've always been interested in my subject. Here are my conclusions. Some men are born good. They grow up to be saints, or heroes, or preachers, or ideal husbands, as the case may be. Maurice Austin Mullins, however, was born bad. Very bad indeed. I like to be very well-dressed, to feel very comfortable in a very big car, with the knowledge that if it breaks down, I have seven others just as big to choose from. I like to buy for every woman I like, everything she likes. I like caviare, and I like champagne. Not because I enjoy the stuff, but because it's so damnably, so gloriously, expensive. Anybody can forge a cheque, anybody can seduce a defenceless female. That's where my artist touch comes in. The good men have their code of sport; I have mine. The little nobodies seduce their women, and marry them because they haven't the courage of their convictions; I give a woman a hell of a good time, and then I cut, clean. The little nobodies forge their cheque with a trembling hand and a sidelong eye, in the quiet of their bedrooms; I forge mine in public, with a flourish, as if I were signing a letter bequeathing a thousand pounds to the Girls' Friendly Society. I've been fulfilling my destiny ever since I extracted chocolates from slot machines with incredible ingenuity. I've been borrowing money, stealing money, and marrying money ever since I can remember. I don't take furtive sniffs at the cup of vice. I drink it to the dregs, with a gesture. I am the Complete Criminal.

Miss Groze. Please listen—please . . .

Mullins. Think of the stake! Two million pounds . . . Think of the danger! That attracts me enormously. In my time I've dabbled a dirty finger in nearly every pie, but never this!

Miss Groze. But that will . . .

Mullins (*still to the audience*) Exactly! The danger! The incredible danger! They'll turn that will on me like a great devastating searchlight. The probability of my having done it will be so enormous they'll *know* I did it, but I'll do it in such a way they can never prove it! You watch me win . . . (*He sits beside her again and looks into her eyes*) Like—to see me—win?

Miss Groze (*after a pause, mesmerized*) Yes . . .

Mullins. Is there a doctor near the theatre?

Miss Groze (*nodding, as if dazed*) Yes, there is . . .

Mullins. So long as he'll be in time to say that life was extinct, as the papers say, before eleven o'clock. . . .

Miss Groze. You're mad—Austin . . .

Mullins (*looking at his watch*) A quarter to ten. Ha! . . . (*Rising and walking about*) My pulse is as steady as a baby's. Those cocktails have put me right on my feet.

Miss Groze. Is there nothing you're afraid of?

Mullins (*with a laugh*) Nothing human.

Miss Groze (*with a start*) Nothing—human!

Mullins (*carelessly*) What?

Miss Groze. Never mind.

Mullins (*going back to her*) Did you find anything useful among her papers?

Miss Groze (*producing a letter from her attaché case*) I think this looks the sort of thing you wanted.

Mullins (*taking it*) Why, we've got the devil's own luck! It's typewritten!

MISS GROZE. Yes. A love-letter she got from an undergraduate when she was at Newnham.

MULLINS. So I see. (*Reading*) "My darling Beatrice, you've told me you love me . . . I believe you." (*Reading a little further*) I say! These schoolboy affairs sound so much worse than they really are, don't they? Signed "Curly". A nickname . . . Good!

MISS GROZE. Well?

MULLINS. Who's the boy friend?

MISS GROZE. He came here about half-past eight and pretended he was a reporter. May be her lover for all I know.

MULLINS. Fits in perfectly. Does my titled relative trust his young wife?

MISS GROZE. He's very fond of her, yes.

MULLINS. My impression is that she likes her old professor of a husband, but that her mother, the dragon woman, married her to him for filthy lucre. And her heart could very easily be elsewhere. Am I right?

MISS GROZE. I think so.

MULLINS. Fits in perfectly.

MISS GROZE. But I don't see what you're driving at . . .

MULLINS. Then *wait* and see! Watch me stage a first-class family squabble, guaranteed to explode in rather less than five minutes! First of all—it's dated nineteen-twenty-seven—off with the date. . . . Who's that moving out there? (*He tears off a corner of the letter and puts away the corner in his breast pocket*)

MISS GROZE (*looking out beyond the right of the archway*) Mrs Arthur.

MULLINS. The dragon woman . . . (*He whips the letter into Jasper's book and lays it on the small table*) Glasses!

(*They put on their spectacles again*)

Now watch! (*Calling*) Mrs Arthur!

MRS ARTHUR (*in the wings*) Did you call me, Mr Mullins?

MULLINS. Could you spare a second? Thirty-two . . . Thirty-three . . .

(MRS ARTHUR *comes in from the right of the archway in a short dressing-gown and an elaborate white wig*)

MISS GROZE. Why did you skip twenty-nine?

MULLINS. Did I? I don't think so . . . So I did. Thank you so much, Miss—er——

MISS GROZE. Groze.

MULLINS. Groze . . . I'm so sorry.

MRS ARTHUR. I was on my way to the wardrobe. Do you like my wig?

MULLINS (*looking up at her*) Little Bo-peep—where are your sheep? Can I be your crook?

MRS ARTHUR (*girlishly*) Oh, Mr Mullins! Anything I can do?

MULLINS. Oh, Mrs Arthur, only that book about ghosts . . .
MRS ARTHUR. Oh, dear, Mr Mullins, you don't want to read
that horrible book on a night of celebration!
MULLINS. But I do. It interests me.
MRS ARTHUR. Well, it *was* here . . . Oh, yes, there it is.
MULLINS. Yes . . .

(*He waits for her to take it up. She is toying with her wig*)

Er—which is the best chapter to start on?
MRS ARTHUR. Well . . . (*She takes up the book, opens it, reads the
letter, shuts the book with a bang, and puts it down on the table again*)
Good heavens!
MULLINS. Bad news?
MRS ARTHUR. But this is monstrous. . . . Miss Groze, will you
please tell Mr James North I want to see him! At once!
MISS GROZE (*rising*) Certainly, Mrs Arthur. (*Going out to the
right of the archway, calling*) Mr North! Mr North!
MULLINS. Mrs Arthur—I'm so sorry—can I be of any . . .?
MRS ARTHUR. Mr Mullins—(*almost beside herself*) my daughter
—my daughter . . .
MULLINS. A love letter?
MRS ARTHUR. Unmistakably.
MULLINS. Oh, but it may be a perfectly harmless affair. After
all, we're all innocent until we're proved guilty . . .
MRS ARTHUR. Mr Mullins, it's no use your shielding either of
them. This letter catches them. Flagrantly!

(JIMMY *comes in from the right of the archway, his collar and tie
undone and wearing no coat or waistcoat*)

JIMMY (*brightly*) Did I hear Miss Groze call up for me?
MRS ARTHUR. Leave this house—I mean this theatre!
JIMMY. But . . .
MULLINS (*putting up his feet on the sofa, enjoying himself to the full*)
Now, now, my dear Mrs Arthur, really, really . . .
MRS ARTHUR. How dare you carry on a vulgar intrigue with
my daughter?
JIMMY. How dare you insinuate that your daughter could be
vulgar if she tried?
MRS ARTHUR. I do insinuate! She *has* got mixed up in a vulgar
intrigue!
JIMMY. I hate to contradict a lady, but she has not!
MRS ARTHUR. She has!
JIMMY. She has not! I know her better than you do!
MRS ARTHUR. You don't!
JIMMY. I do!
MRS ARTHUR. You don't!
JIMMY. You get the first prize for bickering.
MULLINS. Now, now, keep the peace, keep the peace . . .

(BEATRICE *hurries on from the right of the archway, in a négligée*)

BEATRICE (*coming down and joining them*) What's all this shouting, everybody?

MULLINS. I think I'd better go . . .

MRS ARTHUR. No, Mr Mullins, please stay, you're one of the family and justice must follow its course . . .

BEATRICE. Mr North, what is all this about?

MRS ARTHUR. Mr North indeed! You mean—(*flourishing the letter dramatically*) Curly!

JIMMY. Curly!

(BEATRICE *leans forward and reads the letter*)

MRS ARTHUR. In a book you've been reading!

BEATRICE (*smiling*) But—this is absurd! This is a letter I got from a stupid young man when I was at college . . .

JIMMY (*looking*) It isn't my handwriting either . . .

MRS ARTHUR. It's typewritten! It's a vulgar intrigue!

BEATRICE. Mother! I don't know this gentleman!

MRS ARTHUR. You do. (*Looking from one to the other, ponderously*) Well.

JIMMY. And now we know where we stand.

MRS ARTHUR. We do not!

JIMMY. There you go again!

MRS ARTHUR. Beatrice, your conduct strikes me dumb . . .

JIMMY. It does not!

MRS ARTHUR. Beatrice, are you aware that you are married, and rather well married at that?

MULLINS. And divorce, I think, is such a disgrace . . .

MRS ARTHUR. As far as I am concerned, divorce is a headline in the Sunday newspapers and no more!

JIMMY. Yes, but you take jolly good care to read the paragraphs underneath! We might have known each other for years, mightn't we?

BEATRICE. You need never be afraid of divorce, Mother. There's one person whom I don't want to hurt . . .

MRS ARTHUR. Don't be thinking of me.

JIMMY. She's not.

BEATRICE. I don't want Charles to think I've just used his money, and played him a filthy trick . . .

MRS ARTHUR. It strikes me the filthy trick has been played already.

(*A pause*)

BEATRICE⎱
JIMMY ⎰(*together*) What do you mean?

MRS ARTHUR. I have a certain knowledge of life, thank you.

JIMMY (*bearing down upon her, in a crescendo of anger*) Mrs Arthur, that remark forfeits any claim you may have to my respect as

Lady Jasper's mother. I've never told a woman what I thought of her, but I'm afraid I'm going to tell you. You've married your daughter for money. Do you know what you are? You're an immoral adventuress!

MRS ARTHUR. What!

(JASPER *comes hurrying in from the right of the archway. He is still in his dinner-jacket*)

JASPER. Hullo!

MRS ARTHUR. Charles!

JASPER. Is anyone hurt?

MRS ARTHUR. Yes!

JASPER. Who?

MRS ARTHUR. I am!

JASPER. Oh, my dear! Where?

MRS ARTHUR. Don't be absurd!

JASPER. My dear, do explain!

MRS ARTHUR. Charles, please order this—gentleman off this stage at once!

JASPER. Really? (*Peering into the orchestra pit*) Cavendish! Cavendish . . . No, there's nobody to hear . . .

MRS ARTHUR (*as he looks at Mullins a little doubtfully*) It's all right, Charles, Mr Mullins is one of the family . . .

BEATRICE (*smiling again*) Charles, it's that ridiculous letter . . .

JASPER. What letter?

MRS ARTHUR (*suddenly confused*) Oh, that—that's nothing, Charles dear . . . The point is, that I have been grossly insulted by an insufferable young boor . . .

MULLINS (*to Jimmy*) That's you.

BEATRICE. Charles, will you please look at that letter?

MRS ARTHUR (*more and more confused*) No, no . . . That's really nothing, Charles dear . . .

JASPER (*taking the letter from her and looking at it*) Excuse me.

MULLINS. My dear Sir Charles, I'm sure it's all a silly mistake and everybody can be good friends again . . .

JASPER (*seriously*) Beatrice, this is a love letter.

BEATRICE. Somebody wrote it to me three years ago.

MULLINS. And Mrs Arthur was rash enough to jump to a thoroughly embarrassing conclusion about this thoroughly innocuous young man . . .

MRS ARTHUR. No, Mr Mullins, I—well . . .

MULLINS. Now, I don't want to interfere in what doesn't concern me, but I do want to see justice done. Why, these young people have known each other for years.

(*A pause*)

BEATRICE. But we haven't . . . We met last week for a second, and again tonight!

MULLINS. Oh—I'm sorry . . .

JIMMY (*furious*) What made you think that?

MULLINS. Well—er—I hope I'm not making trouble—but your saying you knew Lady Jasper better than her own mother did.

JASPER (*after a pause*) Oh.

BEATRICE. But we *did* only meet last week!

(JASPER *looks to Jimmy for an explanation*)

JIMMY (*completely flummoxed*) I meant—that I understood Lady Jasper's character—better than some people did, in spite of the fact I—I've only just met her, and . . .

JASPER (*slowly and ironically*) I—see . . .

MULLINS. I'm so sorry if I've put my foot in it—but really, Mr North's calling here tonight perfectly innocently . . .

JASPER. But now I come to think of it—he didn't . . . He came here in the most furtive manner possible, disguised as a reporter who couldn't remember his own name.

MRS ARTHUR (*sitting down, and getting quite alarmed*) But, Charles dear, Beatrice, I am sure, is . . .

BEATRICE (*going up to her husband, very seriously*) Charles, I have never been unfaithful to you, and I have no intention of being unfaithful to you now . . . (*After a pause*) Charles, don't you believe me?

JASPER (*mildly*) My dear . . . (*He shrugs his shoulders and turns away*)

MRS ARTHUR. Oh, Charles, how can you!

BEATRICE (*stung*) Charles, that's rather caddish!

JASPER. I'm not an attractive husband, and unfortunately my fortieth birthday won't make me any more attractive.

MULLINS. I'm sure that when Mr North has explained his quixotic idea in coming here in disguise . . .

BEATRICE. Charles, you ought not to need any explanation. You ought to know me better than that!

JASPER. I'm very fond of you, my dear. Unfortunately I'm a philosopher as well. So I was more or less prepared for a— well . . . (*He shrugs his shoulders again*)

BEATRICE. Oh!

JIMMY (*in a furious whisper*) How dare you!

BEATRICE. No! I'll speak for myself! Charles, I was too young to know it at the time, but I married you for your money . . .

MRS ARTHUR. Beatrice!

BEATRICE (*to her, in a blaze*) *You* ought to know . . . I've always been fond of you. I've never loved you . . . But if you knew how I've tried to be fair! And *been* fair too, much fairer than you deserved! And now, for you, all that means absolutely nothing against this stupid mistake! Well, I'd sooner starve than be treated as you've treated me in the last two minutes! I'm leaving you tonight!

(BEATRICE *rushes out to the right of the archway, shaking with anger*)

MULLINS. My dear Sir Charles, this is extremely painful . . .

MRS ARTHUR (*rising in a panic*) Leaving you! Oh—but—I'll talk her round, Charles dear . . . This is absurd . . . Beatrice . . . Beatrice, dear!

(*She hurries after Beatrice.* JIMMY *makes to follow her*)

JASPER. And where are you going, young man?

JIMMY (*bitterly*) Home.

(JIMMY *goes out to the right of the archway. The two are left together at last. A pause.* MULLINS *rises, puts his papers on the floor, and goes to the back of the sofa.* JASPER *is a little shaken*)

MULLINS. I'm really extremely sorry, Sir Charles . . .

JASPER. It'll blow over, it'll blow over. She won't leave. I knew I should have to cope with this situation sooner or later, she's very young, Mr Mullins . . . Oh, dear . . . (*He has taken up his book mechanically and sat on the sofa, and is turning over the leaves*)

MULLINS. It's shaken you up, just the same. Now, I tell you what, Sir Charles! You sit here, and have ten minutes' complete rest before the others come down.

JASPER. Well . . .

MULLINS. I'll see you're not disturbed.

JASPER. Well, that's very nice of you. I think I will . . . And what are you going to do?

MULLINS (*with a start*) Me? Oh—I'll get on with my short story.

JASPER (*gradually getting immersed in his reading*) Good . . .

(*A pause.* MULLINS *looks at him carefully, puts his papers on the small table, sees a bell fixed on it, goes up to the archway, looks out cautiously, crosses to the door, and opens it.*

MISS GROZE *stands in the doorway, the picture of fear*)

MULLINS (*looking into her eyes*) Miss Groze . . . That bell, can you hear it from upstairs?

(MISS GROZE *nods*)

Sir Charles is resting. See that nobody comes down on the stage till I ring that bell.

(MISS GROZE *nods and goes. A pause.* MULLINS *studies the ceiling, peers into the orchestra pit, opens the curtains over the alcove, examines the alcove, goes to the foot of the supper-table, takes a tiny bottle from his waistcoat pocket, takes a pill out of it, replaces the pill in one pocket and the bottle in another, puts an open penknife and a pencil on the small table, winds a red-stained handkerchief round his right hand, sits in the armchair, and gives a gasp of pain*)

JASPER (*putting down his book and rising*) Good Lord! What have you—why, you've been bleeding like the dickens! Sharpening a pencil, eh? How do you feel?

MULLINS. I—I'm afraid I can't stand the sight of blood . . . I feel faint . . .

JASPER (*crossing to the sideboard and pouring out a whisky and soda*) Have a drink.

MULLINS. No.

JASPER. You must! It'll pull you together!

MULLINS. No, really . . .

JASPER. Yes!

MULLINS. Well—if you insist.

JASPER. That's right. (*He puts the whisky and soda on the small table near Mullins*) I tell you what (*going back to the sideboard*)—I'll keep you company!

MULLINS (*as* JASPER *pours out another whisky and soda*) Good!

JASPER. What a very nasty little accident! Especially if you're a bit squeamish.

MULLINS. Quite.

(JASPER *comes back to the small table carrying his drink*)

MULLINS. It's a damned nuisance. I've simply got to get this story off before midnight . . . (*Stopping him as he is about to drink*) Oh, Sir Charles! Would—would you mind sorting out these loose pages for me?

JASPER. Certainly. Anything to help a brother author. Mr Mullins! Twenty-seven, twenty-eight . . .

(MULLINS *cautiously takes the pill from his pocket and his hand slowly creeps towards the other's glass*)

Twenty-nine, thirty, thirty-one . . . (*Turning to him*) Is it a good story?

MULLINS (*his hand shooting back like lightning*) Ye-es. It's a bit melodramatic. You'll love the end.

JASPER. Thirty-two, thirty-three.

(*With one convulsive jerk*, MULLINS *drops the pill into the other's glass*)

Thirty-four, thirty-five—I've come to the end.

MULLINS. Have—have you?

JASPER (*putting down the papers and lifting his glass*) Well, here's to an hysterical little wife for whom I have a great affection! (*Putting his glass to his lips and then drawing it away again*) Here's to your very good health, my only living relative! (*Doing the same again*) And for your sake, may it be long before that clock strikes eleven! (*He drinks, and grimaces a little*) Tastes a bit sharp. What about yours?

MULLINS. Oh, mine's all right . . . (*As if suddenly on the point of losing his nerve, he gulps his drink quickly*)

JASPER. My palate, probably . . . (*Sitting on the sofa*) See if you can write now.

(MULLINS *tries. The pen slips through his fingers*)

MULLINS. Damn!

JASPER. I know . . . I'll be your secretary! You dictate the rest to me, and I'll take it down! (*He flourishes the pen and examines the sheets of the manuscript*)

MULLINS. I say, this is most terribly kind of you. Let me see . . . Where did I leave off?

JASPER (*reading in a sing-song voice*) "The door opened with a creak of protestation." That's rather good style, isn't it? Er— "Sylvia stood on the threshold in a radiant new frock, new paragraph. Why, child, exclaimed her sister, after a strained pause, where have you been? I've been and got married, said Sylvia, sitting down proudly full stop."

MULLINS. New paragraph. (*Dictating*) "Married, gasped Dorothy, 'but,' dash, 'but,' again—but, but why? Because, said Sylvia with a catch in her voice, because you forbade me to go to Paris . . ."

JASPER. Forbade?

MULLINS. Forbade, forbad, I don't mind. "Forbade me to go to Paris for my holiday with Peter." Too fast?

JASPER. She does sound a bit modern, yes . . .

MULLINS. "And then . . ."

JASPER. End of the page.

MULLINS. Damn, I haven't any more paper.

JASPER. Oh. That's all right! Miss Groze has some of my note-paper here. I'll use that. (*He takes a sheet from the table*) "Paris for my holiday with Peter."

MULLINS. Er . . . (*Dictating very carefully, while* JASPER *repeats after him in a mumble*) "My dear . . . I've done this . . . because what you've done . . . is the unkindest thing . . . that has ever happened to me. I'm not mad exclamation mark . . . Good luck comma . . . Good-bye."

JASPER. Good strong dialogue. I congratulate you.

MULLINS. Would you mind reading out that last bit?

JASPER (*putting down the rest of the papers and reading from the note-paper, ponderously*) "My dear, I've done this because what you've done is the unkindest thing that has ever happened to me. I'm not mad! Good luck, good-bye." By Jove! (*He looks up slowly, as if he suddenly felt inexplicable pain*)

MULLINS (*watching him*) Full stop . . .

(JASPER *sways to his feet, clutching the paper in his right hand; he is gradually seized by convulsive spasms of pain.* MULLINS *has risen too.*

Suddenly JASPER *looks up, and sees before him the cool smiling face of his murderer. A slow look of horror and understanding creeps into his eyes, and he gives a cry)*

JASPER. I—I—I—(*his voice is throttled*) you're after the money—but—I'll beat you—I'll beat you—I . . .

(*He staggers after* MULLINS, *who retreats quickly into the alcove.* JASPER *follows him, and after terrible convulsions falls dead in the armchair in the alcove, his left hand hanging out of the window, the piece of paper clutched in his other hand*)

MULLINS. Phew! (*He stands back and looks at the dead body for a moment. He listens carefully to the dead man's heart, tests his breathing with a pocket mirror, takes out the bottle of pills and puts it, with Jasper's glass, by the dead body, wrapping them in his handkerchief to avoid fingerprints. He is about to close the curtains when he starts suddenly*) The white carnation . . .

(*He closes the curtains with a violent jerk. He cleans out and puts away his own glass on the sideboard, puts away the handkerchief, knife, and pencil in his pocket, sits in the armchair and goes on with his short story. The clock strikes ten. He listens.*

BEATRICE *appears noiselessly from the right of the archway, dressed in white, in the costume of Dante's Beatrice, and sees him*)

MULLINS (*rising, with uncontrollable and childish joy*) My God, what an adventure!

BEATRICE. What did you say?

(MULLINS *gives a violent start, collects himself, and turns to her*)

MULLINS. How charming you look.

BEATRICE. What did you say before that?

MULLINS. I was wondering exactly what the hero of my next short story is going to say when he sights the skyscrapers of New York.

BEATRICE. Oh.

MULLINS. Do you think "My God, what an adventure!" is plausible?

BEATRICE. Most, I should say.

MULLINS. No. I think I prefer the original.

BEATRICE. What was that?

MULLINS. "My God, why did I leave London?"

BEATRICE. Oh . . . Have you seen Mrs Wragg?

MULLINS. I've been too busy to see anybody.

BEATRICE. Too busy?

MULLINS. Oh . . . On my immortal work.

BEATRICE. I wonder if Mrs Wragg's dressed up yet . . .

(MRS WRAGG *comes in from the right of the archway, dressed in white, as Katherine Parr, carrying a tray of six cocktails*)

MRS WRAGG. Not 'arf.

MULLINS. Would you like me to look for this Wragg person for you?

MRS WRAGG (*witheringly*) This Wragg person is already havailable, thank you very much all the same! Supper's ready, my lady, though cooking utensils in the basement of this 'ere theatre of such a temporairy nature I never saw.

BEATRICE. I'm so sorry, Mrs Wragg! How do you feel?

MRS WRAGG. Not so bad, my lady, considering it's all 'istorical. I could deal all right with me 'oops and me loops, but I met me Waterloo with me farthin'-jale.

MULLINS (*tentatively*) Farthin Gale . . .?

MRS WRAGG (*finally*) Farthin Jale.

MULLINS (*to Beatrice*) Turned a bit cold, hasn't it? We shall meet again anon . . . I'll now go and find what Ghost of History is most worthy that I should represent him—or it, as the case may be! (*To Mrs Wragg*) *Au revoir, chère Madame* Wragg! *A toute à l'heure*, great Catherine of all the Russias!

(MULLINS *goes out to the right of the archway, with a flourish*)

MRS WRAGG (*beside herself, after him*) Bloody Mary to you! Beg pardon, my lady, but that man frays my nerves.

BEATRICE (*sitting on the edge of the armchair*) I didn't know you'd seen him before, Mrs Wragg.

MRS WRAGG. I met him coming in through the stage door, all dressed up to the nines . . . How dare 'e speak French to me!

BEATRICE. But—why don't you like him?

MRS WRAGG (*arranging the supper-table*) 'Ate at first sight, my lady. That is not a nice man to know. And if you say he is till you're blue, I shall still say, "That is not a nice man to know."

BEATRICE. But you've only seen him for a second!

MRS WRAGG (*with great conviction*) It's 'is eyes. I always judges by eyes.

BEATRICE. Oh—that's rather interesting . . .

MRS WRAGG. I 'ates to contradict my Bible, my lady, but that is a neighbour of mine as I will *not* love. Moses 'ad never 'eard of this one.

BEATRICE. How is it that when that man is standing there in front of me, I almost like him, and as soon as he's out of sight, I loathe him? Isn't it strange?

MRS WRAGG. The only strange thing about it, my lady, is that you almost like 'im when 'e's standing there in front of you! That's the time I 'ate 'im most.

BEATRICE. And yet . . .

MRS WRAGG (*going up to her, brandishing her tray*) My advice to you, my lady, if I may make so audacious, is this, short and sharp. 'Ate 'im. And when you've finished 'ating 'im—start again . . . Well, my lady, we've got no ghost to be frightened of after all! And now you can enjoy the party in peace. (*Going towards the door*)

BEATRICE. Mrs Wragg!

MRS WRAGG. Yes, my lady?

BEATRICE. I—I've always thought you understood things so much better than the people I meet . . .

MRS WRAGG (*flattered*) Yes, my lady.

BEATRICE. Well, Mrs Wragg. I'm going away tomorrow morning.

MRS WRAGG (*coming back to her*) Away, my lady? For your 'ealth?

BEATRICE (*smiling*) Yes, for my health . . . Mrs Wragg . . .

(*She motions MRS WRAGG to sit in the armchair, and sits on the arm of it herself*)

I'm going to ask you something I've always been dying to know . . What do you think of my husband?

MRS WRAGG (*reluctantly*) 'E's all right, my lady.

BEATRICE. I'm going to leave him, tomorrow.

MRS WRAGG. Leave him, my lady?

BEATRICE. My mother, you see, makes things . . .

MRS WRAGG. If you don't mind me sayin' so, my lady, your mother an' me don't what you might call kiss each other neither, even on Sundays.

BEATRICE. He and mother accused me of—something rather unjust, so I called him a cad, so . . .

MRS WRAGG (*horrified*) Called him a cad! . . . My lady, if I may make so audacious, that was a nasty thing to do!

BEATRICE. Oh!

MRS WRAGG. Yes, my lady, nasty! And excessively unlike you, excessively!

BEATRICE. But . . .

MRS WRAGG. He's that fond of you, my lady! 'Ave a good 'eart to 'eart talk with 'im, and come to a real understanding, one way or the other!

BEATRICE. You think I'm a coward?

MRS WRAGG. Only cowards run away, my lady.

BEATRICE (*rising, thoughtfully*) He *has* been good to me, in his funny way . . .

MRS WRAGG (*rising*) It's not too late. If 'usband and wife must part, they might as well part in friendship as in animanity . . . I'll call 'im.

BEATRICE. Just go to his dressing-room and tell him I want to speak to him.

MRS WRAGG (*suddenly stopping*) But 'e wasn't there this very minute as ever was, my lady. 'E's on the stage, I expect, fiddling with lights. I'll go round this 'ere scenery and 'ave a look. (*She makes to go to the right opening*)

BEATRICE. Oh, and—Mrs Wragg! On your way round, will you go to the switch-board and turn off these lights, and leave on the special lights we arranged for the party?

MRS WRAGG. Yes, my lady.

(MRS WRAGG *goes out through the right opening.* BEATRICE *lights the candles on the supper-table. Most of the lights go out. Weird candle-light. Beyond the archway there is now almost complete darkness.* BEATRICE *sits in the armchair*)

(*Going round the set*) He's not on this side, my lady . . .

(*She is seen crossing the archway*)

He's over 'ere, I expect, though I don't see 'ow . . .

(*Her voice suddenly dies behind the alcove. A pause, and then a clatter of footsteps. She appears through the left opening, rather frightened*)

My lady—the window of this 'ere alcove is a bit open—and—and there's a hand pointing out of it—with a signet ring on it—and—and some initials on the ring . . .

BEATRICE. C. J.—Charles Jasper . . .

MRS WRAGG. Oh, yes, of course . . . (*Trying hard to reassure herself*) Yes . . .

BEATRICE. Whatever can he be doing there? (*Knitting her brows, uneasily*) He must have fallen asleep. Perhaps he wasn't so upset after all . . . Wake him, will you, Mrs Wragg?

MRS WRAGG. Yes, my lady. (*She opens the right half of the curtains. The dead body . . . She stands staring a moment, then utters a low sharp cry*) Oh, my lady . . .

(BEATRICE *starts, turns and rises with a gasp*)

BEATRICE (*running to the alcove*) He's fainted . . . (*She gives one look at the distorted face, feels the heart mechanically, falls on her knees beside the body, and stares at it frantically. Dully*) He's dead.

MRS WRAGG. Oh . . .

BEATRICE. What's—what's that little bottle there . . . (*With a shudder*) Poison! (*She sees the letter clasped in the hand, takes it, and reads it. A pause. She suddenly closes the curtains on the dead body and sinks into the armchair, the letter clutched in her hand. In a hard voice*) I've got to work this out.

MRS WRAGG (*coming down, dazed*) Shall I—telephone for the police?

BEATRICE. We mustn't send for anybody!

MRS WRAGG. Not—not send for anybody?

(BEATRICE *looks frantically into her face.* MRS WRAGG *understands that she means what she has said*)

BEATRICE. Nobody's seen us?

MRS WRAGG. They're still up there. There isn't a soul about

. . . (*Losing control of herself, crying*) Oh, this is a terrible thing to 'ave 'appened, terrible, terrible . . .

BEATRICE (*suddenly quite hysterical*) Stop, stop, stop!

(*She is beating the arms of her chair with her fists.* MRS WRAGG *suddenly becomes as calm as a stone*)

MRS WRAGG (*putting her arms round her*) That's all right . . . Shh . . . My pretty—it's all right, dear . . . It's all right . . .

BEATRICE (*sobbing*) I've never seen—anybody—dead before . . .

MRS WRAGG. Shhh . . . It's all right . . .

BEATRICE (*hard again*) No. It's not all right.

MRS WRAGG. No. It's all—very much wrong . . .

BEATRICE. Then—then you feel it too?

MRS WRAGG. Your 'usband 'asn't died a natural manner of dyin'.

BEATRICE. I know! Poison!

MRS WRAGG. I mean more than that. Somebody 'elped 'im to 'is death.

BEATRICE. But this is a letter of suicide!

MRS WRAGG. Suicide? (*With immense emphasis*) Never! 'E never felt things bad enough for that, never! He was the last man on God's earth to do such a thing!

BEATRICE. But—his own handwriting!

MRS WRAGG. It's a forgery.

BEATRICE. But how do you know?

(MRS WRAGG *makes a gesture of impotence*)

Did you really draw that curtain just now? Is he really lying behind there—dead? (*Controlling herself*) Can't you help me?

MRS WRAGG (*staring in front of her, suddenly*) It's 'is eyes.

BEATRICE (*mechanically*) His eyes?

MRS WRAGG. Yes. I'm sure that's it. It's 'is eyes.

BEATRICE. Whose eyes?

MRS WRAGG. That fellow what went out just now!

(BEATRICE *gives a violent start and looks at her. A pause*)

BEATRICE. Mrs Wragg, you don't think . . .?

MRS WRAGG. I believe!

BEATRICE. Yes . . . I can see his eyes . . . It *is* his eyes! Smiling . . . A man with eyes like that would do anything to steal a fortune . . .

MRS WRAGG. A fortune? Whose fortune?

BEATRICE. That man is Maurice Mullins.

MRS WRAGG. Maurice Mu—Maurice Mullins! (*She rushes to the telephone*)

BEATRICE. And in less than an hour . . .

MRS WRAGG (*taking up the receiver*) What's the number of Scotland Yard?

BEATRICE (*rising quickly and seizing her by the hands*) You can't have a man arrested for murder because you don't like the look of his eyes!

(MRS WRAGG *nods hopelessly and puts down the telephone.* BEATRICE *sits*)

BEATRICE (*suddenly*) I've got it!

MRS WRAGG. Yes?

BEATRICE. When I came in he was standing there, then he cried, "My God, what an adventure!" . . . He did it!

MRS WRAGG. I know 'e did, my dear, but even that ain't good enough proof . . .

BEATRICE. Then it means we've got to find proof.

MRS WRAGG. Send for a detective! Send that there Miss Groze!

BEATRICE (*in an inspiration*) Miss Groze! (*She presses the bell on the table*)

MRS WRAGG. But . . .

BEATRICE. We've got to go on perfectly ordinarily, as if—as if nothing had happened . . .

MRS WRAGG (*half turning fearfully to the curtained alcove*) But . . .

BEATRICE. It's monstrous, I know, but we've got to do it . . .

(*She puts the letter away in a pouch on her dress, takes up a journal from the small table, sits on the sofa, and turns over the leaves.* MRS WRAGG *goes up stage, and stands staring at the black curtains, as if mesmerized.*

MISS GROZE *comes in from the door, dressed in a white costume, as Mary Queen of Scots. She is as impassive as ever. She sees Mrs Wragg staring at the curtains and starts. She comes down to Beatrice.* MRS WRAGG *crosses to the supper-table. The following conversation is very quickly and—apparently—casually conducted on both sides*)

BEATRICE (*turning over pages*) I'm sorry to trouble you, but do you know where my mother is?

MISS GROZE. She's changing in her dressing-room.

BEATRICE. Cavendish?

MISS GROZE. Still eating.

BEATRICE. Mr North?

MISS GROZE. He hasn't gone yet.

BEATRICE. Austin?

MISS GROZE. He was in the top dressing-room a minute ago brushing his hair.

BEATRICE. Thank you, Miss Groze . . .

(MISS GROZE *turns to go*)

(*Very casually*) Oh, Miss Groze!

Miss Groze (*turning back*) Lady Jasper?
Beatrice (*rising and going very close to her*) Miss Groze—how did you know Mr Mullins's second name was Austin?

(*A long pause.* Miss Groze *is staring in front of her. She does not flinch for the flicker of an eyelid*)

Miss Groze (*at last*) I beg your pardon, Lady Jasper?
Beatrice. You heard perfectly the first time. Well?

(Miss Groze *turns to her. They look into each other's eyes, their fists clenched. It is a little battle of wits*)

Miss Groze. I don't see what Austin has to do with Mr Mullins, Lady Jasper, if I may say so. All I know is that Austin was in Mr Mullins's dressing-room when I was passing just now.
Beatrice. Will you please explain yourself, Miss Groze?
Miss Groze. Why, Lady Jasper, Austin is the name of the theatre cat. I christened it last week, the day we came to look over the theatre with Sir Charles.
Beatrice. Oh. And why did you christen it Austin?
Miss Groze (*after the fraction of a pause*) Because it was standing on the bonnet of an Austin Seven outside the stage door.
Beatrice. Oh.
Miss Groze. There was a kitten as well, which I christened the Baby Austin.
Beatrice. I see. You embroider very cleverly indeed, Miss Groze. And how do you account for Austin brushing his hair?
Miss Groze (*after the fraction of a pause*) I said washing his fur, Lady Jasper.
Beatrice. Oh.
Miss Groze. Why, Lady Jasper, even if I did know Mr Mullins's Christian names, I should never dream of calling him by any of them, or mention his brushing his hair, Lady Jasper.
Beatrice. May I suggest, Miss Groze, that you mentioned it because you were absent-minded?
Miss Groze. Certainly, Lady Jasper.
Beatrice. Thank you, Miss Groze.
Miss Groze. Not at all, Lady Jasper. (*She turns to go*)
Beatrice. Miss Groze!
Miss Groze (*turning back again*) Lady Jasper?
Beatrice. You're an extremely clever woman.
Miss Groze. Thank you, Lady Jasper . . . (*She turns up stage*)

(Beatrice *sits in the armchair.* Miss Groze *finds herself face to face with the black curtains. She stands motionless, her back to the footlights*)

(*In a hard strained voice*) Shall I call Sir Charles?

(Mrs Wragg *starts, and exchanges a look with* Beatrice)

BEATRICE (*loudly and calmly*) Not yet, thank you, Miss Groze. My husband has a headache, and asks to be excused . . . Mrs Wragg!

MRS WRAGG. Yes, my lady?

BEATRICE. Will you go and tell the others that supper is ready?

MRS WRAGG (*going up stage towards the archway*) Yes, my lady.

MISS GROZE (*still with her back to them, in the same strained rather shrill voice*) Shall I ring the bell for them?

BEATRICE (*sharply*) No, thank you, Miss Groze. (*She rises*)

MISS GROZE. Very well, Lady Jasper.

(*MISS GROZE goes out to the right of the archway. BEATRICE runs up and looks after her*)

BEATRICE (*urgently*) Tell them all—except Mullins.

MRS WRAGG. Yes . . .

BEATRICE. Tell him that supper won't be on the table for another ten minutes, and I'll ring when it's time. Can you remember that?

MRS WRAGG. I think I can . . . (*Clasping her hands*) Oh, my dear—what is going to 'appen?

BEATRICE. I—I don't know . . .

(*MRS WRAGG presses her hand, and goes out to the right of the archway. BEATRICE looks at the black curtains, and shrinks away from them. She hears somebody outside the door, and stands against the wall behind it. The door opens slowly. MISS GROZE appears. She stares at the curtains as if fascinated, and goes stealthily to them. BEATRICE creeps down just as stealthily to the supper-table. As MISS GROZE is about to draw the curtains, BEATRICE drops a glass with a clatter. MISS GROZE turns with a violent start. A pause. MR CAVENDISH and his band clamber into the orchestra pit*)

MISS GROZE (*coming down to the footlights*) Are you ready, Mr Cavendish?

CAVENDISH. Ready, Miss Groze.

(*MISS GROZE is about to go out by the archway when she meets JIMMY, who comes in from the right of the archway, in white, with hunting-boots and cape, dressed as Henry of Navarre*)

BEATRICE (*seeing him*) But I . . . Miss Groze, would you mind telling my mother that we are waiting?

(*MISS GROZE goes out to the right of the archway*)

BEATRICE (*quickly*) I thought you were going . . .

JIMMY. I thought you were . . .

BEATRICE. I changed my mind . . .

JIMMY. So did I. I don't care if I'm not quite as welcome in this theatre as I might be.

BEATRICE. Why are you staying?

JIMMY. I want to look after you.

BEATRICE. I'm glad you're staying . . . You're—you're—rather a help.

(MRS ARTHUR *comes in from the right of the archway, a magnificent figure in white, as Marie Antoinette. She is followed by* MISS GROZE)

JIMMY. I don't trust that man Mullins.

MRS ARTHUR. The most charming man in the world. Are you a guest here, still?

JIMMY. Permanently.

(*The band begins to play "Zulu Wail", a very slow blues dance, very softly. It seems to affect even* MRS ARTHUR *and* JIMMY *with foreboding.* MRS ARTHUR *crosses very slowly and stands by the lower stool on the right of the supper-table.* BEATRICE *stands at the head of the table,* JIMMY *on her left.* MISS GROZE *makes to stand by the lower seat on the left of the table*)

BEATRICE (*sharply*) Miss Groze, won't you sit here?

(*She indicates her right.* MISS GROZE *hesitates, and stands on Beatrice's right. They all sit. A pause.* MRS WRAGG *comes in from the right of the archway and stands behind Beatrice*)

MRS WRAGG. Shall I serve, my lady?

MRS ARTHUR. But what on earth is Charles doing all this time?

BEATRICE. He's in there——

(*She looks to the alcove.* MRS WRAGG *moves and stands between her and it*)

—resting. He's—he's—don't let's wake him, yet . . .

(*The music drones on. She tries hard to pretend, but it is too much for her. She rises with a sudden cry.* JIMMY *rises*)

It's horrible! Horrible! (*Clutching Jimmy's arm*) Thank God you're here . . .

MRS ARTHUR (*startled*) Beatrice!

(BEATRICE *recovers a little and sits.* JIMMY *sits beside her*)

BEATRICE. I don't know where I am. Perhaps it never happened. Perhaps you are Mary Queen of Scots, Marie Antoinette and Henry of Navarre . . . Nothing seems any more real than anything else. And I'm not Beatrice Jasper, but Dante's Beatrice . . . Don't stop playing! Please go on playing, whatever you do . . .

MRS ARTHUR. Beatrice, you're hiding something from me! (*Rising and crossing to the alcove; suddenly and decisively*) I'm going to call Charles and ask him what it's all about. I . . .

BEATRICE. Wait a minute . . . (*She rises, solemn and calm*) He's dead.

(*The music stops. A stupefied pause.* JIMMY *and* MISS GROZE *rise)*

MRS ARTHUR. Dead . . .

BEATRICE. Do you want me to draw the curtain and show you?

MRS ARTHUR. No, no!

(JIMMY *has crossed to the telephone.* MISS GROZE *edges down stage*)

BEATRICE. What are you doing?

JIMMY. Ringing up a doctor.

BEATRICE. It isn't a case for a doctor. Or the police.

MRS ARTHUR. The police!

BEATRICE. My husband has been murdered.

(*A pause. The band scramble to their feet.* MISS GROZE *makes a wild dash for the archway.* JIMMY *catches her by the wrist*)

JIMMY. Nobody leaves this theatre! All the band go under the stage!

(*They go, quickly.* MISS GROZE, *cowed, goes back to her seat at the supper-table*)

MRS ARTHUR. Beatrice, have you lost your senses?

BEATRICE (*implacably*) My husband was murdered, less than half an hour ago, by somebody who is in this theatre now.

JIMMY. Who?

BEATRICE. Maurice Mullins.

MRS ARTHUR. Maurice—Mullins!

BEATRICE. Yes . . . And we haven't a grain of proof!

MRS ARTHUR. No proof, and your husband's whole fortune going to him? It's obvious to a child . . .

BEATRICE. To a child perhaps. To a jury—(*producing the letter from her dress*) never.

(*She makes to give it to Jimmy.* MRS ARTHUR *snatches it from her and reads it. She starts*)

JIMMY. What does it say?

MRS ARTHUR (*reading*) "I've done this because what you've done is the unkindest thing that has ever happened to me . . ."

JIMMY. The unkindest thing . . . That was the misunderstanding about me!

MRS ARTHUR. It's a forgery.

JIMMY. Forgeries are part of my job . . . I'll soon spot it for you. (*He takes the letter from her, goes in front of the sofa, and holds it under the light*) A forgery needs hours of careful preparation . . . The ink's hardly dry.

(*A pause.* BEATRICE *comes down to him*)

BEATRICE (*entreatingly*) You don't—believe my husband was
—murdered?
JIMMY (*reluctantly*) It certainly looks like—suicide.

(BEATRICE *sinks in the armchair*)

BEATRICE. Mrs Wragg!
MRS WRAGG. Yes, my lady?
BEATRICE (*at the end of her tether*) My husband has committed
suicide, while insane! And the police must be fetched! Our evening at the St James's Theatre is over! Bring down the curtain!
Turn on all the lights! And we'll go and fetch the police! Bring
down this curtain!
MRS WRAGG (*trying to conceal her distress*) Yes, my lady, as
soon as I can . . .

(MRS WRAGG *goes out through the right opening*)

BEATRICE (*rising; almost hysterical again*) Let Maurice Mullins
come downstairs, smiling, and at eleven o'clock let him stand behind the police, smiling, with his filthy two million pounds in a
heap around him, and a dead body in front of him! Send for the
police! Bring down that curtain! Bring down that . . .

(*Almost beside herself, she has run up to the archway. And she has
stopped. A pause. They look and shrink away.
    Out of the blackness beyond the archway a* WOMAN *walks, very
slowly, and comes slowly and noiselessly down towards the footlights.
She is slim and dark, with a strange irregular beauty. Her hands are fine
and long. She is of any age, and is surrounded by an atmosphere of un-
real placidity. She is dressed in a flimsy dark red evening dress, with a
long misty wrap over her shoulders. She stands still, looking out in front
of her, as if sensing the fact that she can walk no farther. She looks at
Jimmy, a look of entreaty on her face. Then, slowly, her hands rise; the
fingers intertwine in varying patterns, first slowly, then rapidly. They fall
again. Silence. She turns and goes slowly back. The wrap falls from her
shoulders and floats to the floor. She walks into the archway, and seems
to melt into the darkness. She is gone as mysteriously as she came.
Silence*)

She must have walked straight down here from the street . . .
JIMMY. But—who is she?
BEATRICE (*coming down towards him*) I don't know . . .
MISS GROZE (*with a sudden cry*) I know!
BEATRICE. Well?
MISS GROZE. It's in that book!
JIMMY. Book?
MISS GROZE. You remember—we thought we saw a—dumb
woman—in those passages—before Johnson rang up to say the
man wasn't murdered in the theatre! That book says a strange

woman will be found, wandering about the place of the murder
... And she was trying to say something, to him! And she
couldn't! This woman is—dumb!

JIMMY (*mechanically*) But if the message said the man wasn't
murdered here at all, but in King Street . . .

MRS ARTHUR. There hasn't been a murder . . .

BEATRICE (*in a loud cry*) But there has been a murder here!

(*Gradually they realize the situation in which they are being
involved*)

MISS GROZE. It can't be true . . .

BEATRICE (*with the calm of real terror*) If it is true, we've got to
have more courage tonight than we've ever had in our lives
before . . . It's all getting mixed up in my mind. (*Clinging to
Jimmy, with an hysterical laugh*) Here we are, the Ghosts of History,
all dressed up—playing at ghosts—but we're waiting—waiting—
waiting for . . .

(*The telephone rings. They stare at it.* BEATRICE *pulls herself
together and takes off the receiver*)

BEATRICE (*into the telephone, in amazement*) What! (*Turning to
the others*) It's Cavendish—the band conductor . . .

MRS ARTHUR. But he was here this very second . . .

BEATRICE. He's speaking from the telephone box opposite the
stage door . . .

(*A pause. From what is being said at the other end she is obviously at
a loss what to do. She gives a long look at the mysterious drapery lying
on the floor, and finally nerves herself to answer*)

I see . . . No, Mr Cavendish, I'm afraid that if your next call is to
Scotland Yard you will be making a bigger fool of yourself even
than you have done already . . . Won't he . . . Charles?

(*The others start violently*)

Oh, yes, I was speaking to—my husband . . . It's quite simple, he
fainted, and I've got so worked up over this ghost nonsense that I
thought he was not only dead, but murdered . . . (*She laughs
desperately into the telephone*) No, you needn't come back . . . We
aren't going on with the party after all, I'm too upset . . .
(*Hanging up, dully*) Good-bye . . . (*She looks at the telephone for a
moment*)

MRS ARTHUR. Well?

(BEATRICE *picks up the scissors from the small table, and with a
savage twist severs the telephone cord*)

(*Shrilly*) But you're deliberately cutting us off from help . . .

MISS GROZE (*running across to her, panic-stricken*) Please let me
go—please let me go . . .

BEATRICE (*clutching her by the shoulders, in a frenzied cry*) Listen to
me! Listen to me, everybody. We know this man murdered my
husband. We've got to prove it. For an hour—just for a thread of
a chance—we've got to put ourselves in the hands of—a terrible
thing . . . We've got to—wait.

(*Silence*)

Do you all promise to stand by me?
JIMMY. Yes . . .
BEATRICE. Miss Groze, are all the doors locked in the audi-
torium?
MISS GROZE. Yes.
BEATRICE. Then go and lock the stage door.
MISS GROZE. Yes . . . (*She falters before the archway, and turns,
almost in tears*) I can't face those corridors . . .
JIMMY. I'll go.
BEATRICE. Wait a minute. (*Pointing to the wrap*) He mustn't see
this. Take it to an empty dressing-room.

(JIMMY *picks it up and goes out through the right of the archway*)

If he is as innocent as the law would say he is, nothing will happen. If he is guilty, we must wait—for whatever happens.

(MISS GROZE *makes a movement as if to creep away*)

(*Sternly*) Do you understand, Miss Groze?
MISS GROZE (*weakly*) Yes . . .
BEATRICE. Come . . .

(*She sits on her stool at the head of the supper-table. The others
follow suit.
JIMMY returns through the right opening, looks at them, and sits
in his place*)

He must not know that we suspect him . . .

(*A pause. They wait, not daring even to turn.*
MULLINS *enters noiselessly from the right of the archway, a re-
splendent figure in a red Renaissance costume. He stands leaning against
the alcove. MISS GROZE sees him and rises convulsively. The others are
unconscious of his presence. BEATRICE looks at her inquiringly*)

MISS GROZE (*staring over the footlights, a desperate message of warning in her voice*) I understand, Lady Jasper . . . He must not
know—that we suspect—him . . .

(MULLINS *smiles, looks mockingly at the black curtains beside him,
and gives a low laugh. They are electrified, but dare not look. MISS
GROZE sits again. BEATRICE looks at her with bitter understanding.
A pause*)

MULLINS. Where's Sir Charles?

BEATRICE. I'm afraid I must apologize for him, Mr Mullins. He hasn't come down yet.

MULLINS (*coming down to them*) Where is he?

(*A pause*)

BEATRICE (*looking him between the eyes*) He must be in his dressing-room.

(MULLINS *surveys them, with a laugh, and takes up his cocktail*)

MULLINS (*drinking*) What a delightful picture! The Ghosts of History! By the way, has anybody guessed whose ghost I am?

(*They watch him, fascinated*)

The ghost of Caesar Borgia—(*taking his host's glass and holding it up to the light before drinking it*) the world-famous poisoner.

CURTAIN

There is now——

AN INTERVAL

of ten minutes.
     The HOUSE-LIGHTS *go out. A loud laugh from the stage.* BEATRICE *appears at the parting of the curtain and crosses to the left. She is followed by* JIMMY.

BEATRICE. I couldn't stand another minute—sitting there—with him . . .
JIMMY. But why . . .?
BEATRICE. Don't you see? He knows that we know—and he knows we're helpless—and he's playing with us! Just for fun!
MULLINS (*behind the curtain*) Lady Jasper!

(*They listen*)

BEATRICE (*with an effort*) Yes, Mr Mullins?
MULLINS. Aren't you going to take this curtain up? It was Sir Charles's orders, you know!

(*They look at each other*)

BEATRICE (*calling*) Mrs Wragg!
MRS WRAGG (*in the wings*) Yes, my lady?
BEATRICE. Take the curtain up, will you?
MRS WRAGG. I thought you wanted it down, my lady!
BEATRICE. I know—but—but we're going on with the party after all . . . And bring some more cocktails, will you?
MRS WRAGG. Yes, my lady.

A pause. The CURTAIN *rises on——*

ACT III

MULLINS *is in the armchair.* MISS GROZE *and* MRS ARTHUR *are seated at the supper-table, in the same attitudes of tense foreboding. A pause.* BEATRICE *and* JIMMY *cross to their places.*

MULLINS (*surveying the theatre*) Ah, that's better. That was a grand idea of your husband's, to have tonight's party with the curtain up, Lady Jasper . . . (*Rising with restless gaiety*) This is romance! Candlelight is the only light for a supper such as this! The wine is so much rubier, so much more like the true gold. . . . A supper of ghosts on the stage, the footlights glimmering in the rosy radiance of the candles, and the great dark of the theatre beyond. . . .

(*A pause. He sits on the lower stool to the left of the table*)

Well, nobody can say I haven't done my best to entertain you . . .

(*The clock chimes half-past ten.* MRS WRAGG *comes in from the right of the archway with a fresh tray of cocktails. She serves each one. There is one glass left on the tray. She is about to go when* BEATRICE *motions her to serve the last glass. She hesitates, and places it before the empty stool at the foot of the table. She goes out through the door, and returns without the tray. A pause*)

I say, you do look depressed . . . Now, look here, if you all don't wake up soon . . .

BEATRICE (*with an effort*) It's the empty theatre, and these costumes, and the candlelight, and everything . . .

MULLINS. Yes. Ghosts!

(*The word seems to echo through the silent theatre. He looks from one to the other*)

A supper of ghosts, on the stage . . . Do you know what this tableau has reminded me of, quite suddenly? It reminds me of a certain banquet—a certain banquet which Macbeth gave . . .

(*His eyes travel round them and rest finally on the stool at the foot of the table. They follow his look*)

That seat—that empty seat—might be the seat that waits for the guest named—Banquo.

(*A pause*)

BEATRICE. And what—what part in the tragedy would be yours?

MULLINS (*rising; flourishing his glass with a gay laugh*) Why,

Macduff! Macduff, the gallant . . . (*He stops, his back to them, face to face with the black curtains of the alcove. He lifts his glass, slowly, as if toasting somebody who is in front of him . . .*) The guileless—warrior!

(*He looks at them. They seem completely under his spell. He smiles, and looks at his wrist-watch. They stiffen*)

Gone half-past ten!

(BEATRICE *rises convulsively. He leans against the right corner of the alcove, and looks boldly into her eyes*)

Sir Charles must have fallen asleep. (*With deadly meaning*) Don't you think—I'd better try—and wake him?

MISS GROZE (*with a stifled cry*) No . . .

(BEATRICE *silences her immediately. They watch him, holding their breath*)

BEATRICE (*returning his look, fighting hard*) Won't you—have another drink?

MULLINS. Lady Jasper, I—quite understand.

(*They start.* BEATRICE *moves out of the group at the table and goes towards him*)

JIMMY. Stay here!

(BEATRICE *crosses slowly to the steps of the alcove. She stands facing Mullins, her hands clutching the parting of the curtains, as if defying him to pass her*)

MULLINS (*with ominous meaning*) You want a few minutes' grace . . . I quite understand.

BEATRICE (*quickly, challenging*) What do you mean?

MULLINS (*as quickly*) You have no particular desire to see your husband at the present moment . . .

BEATRICE. Why?

MULLINS (*shrugging his shoulders; suddenly playful*) But because you had a few words with him earlier in the evening!

(*They relax, and look at one another.* BEATRICE *comes down to the sofa*)

BEATRICE. Of course . . .

MULLINS. You've got to face him some time. I'm going to wake him . . .

BEATRICE (*desperately, almost in a cry*) Mr Mullins! You said you —acted quite a lot . . . Before I was married—I acted quite a lot too. Talking of Shakespeare, I played Juliet once. I've got rather a jolly photograph . . .

MULLINS (*ironically*) I'd give anything to see it.

BEATRICE. Well, I think it'll be in a suitcase—or lying about somewhere in my dressing-room . . . I think you'll find it.

(MULLINS *laughs, looks from one to the other, and then looks again at his watch*)

(*Turning and facing him again, bitterly*) He'll be here when you come down again.

MULLINS (*with a laugh*)   There's really heaps of time. I'll go and get it . . .

(*As he turns,* MISS GROZE *glides up to him*)

BEATRICE (*sharply*)   Well?

MULLINS.   What?

MISS GROZE.   I don't think Mr Mullins will want to take his glass upstairs with him . . .

(*She looks for a second into his eyes, a world of entreaty in her own. He returns her look with cool affability, smiles, and gives her his glass, with a royal gesture of dismissal*)

MULLINS.   Thank you. Well, cheer up, everybody! Let your philosophy of life be the same as mine!

MRS ARTHUR.   And what may your philosophy of life be?

MULLINS.   Live—and let live!

(MULLINS *goes out to the right of the archway. Silence*)

BEATRICE (*to Jimmy*)   Run upstairs and lock him in my room!

(JIMMY *gives her a startled look, rises and follows Mullins on tiptoe*)

MRS ARTHUR.   Why did you do that?

BEATRICE.   There isn't any photograph . . .

MRS ARTHUR.   Then . . .

BEATRICE.   Oh, don't you see? It's a breathing space! I couldn't bear it any longer!

MRS ARTHUR (*rising*)   I'll tell him we know the truth . . . I'll tell him we've got evidence! He's bound to make a slip . . .

BEATRICE.   That man has never made a slip in his life!

MRS ARTHUR (*crossing to her, cowed at last*)   Now look here, Beatrice . . . I've given in for the moment to all this superstition, just to give you a fair chance . . . Now are we going to be kept in this agony all night?

BEATRICE (*hopelessly*)   I—I don't know . . . How can I tell . . .?

MRS ARTHUR.   Is—is what you are waiting for—going to happen?

MRS WRAGG.   It is, my lady, it is! What about that woman I saw in the passage . . .

MRS ARTHUR.   And is it going to happen in the next twenty minutes, before that man insists on drawing that curtain?

BEATRICE (*holding her forehead, wearily, stumbling across to the right proscenium arch*)   I don't know . . . I don't know . . .

MRS ARTHUR.   But we've got to prove it, we've got to . . .

(BEATRICE *sinks against the proscenium arch*)

MRS WRAGG. My lady . . .

BEATRICE. Wait! There's somebody moving out here . . .

MRS ARTHUR. It's Mullins.

MISS GROZE (*shrinking past the sofa*) No! It isn't! . . .

(JIMMY *comes in from the right of the archway. He looks back and beckons.*

THE DUMB WOMAN *walks slowly past him, and down the stage. She feels the armchair beside her, hesitates, and sits in it. She is looking calmly in front of her. Silence*)

BEATRICE (*to Jimmy*) But . . .

JIMMY. I met her on the stairs.

BEATRICE. If only you would speak!

MRS ARTHUR (*crossing to her*) Can't you try to tell us . . .?

BEATRICE. If only you would speak! The book says—if only you would speak . . .

MRS ARTHUR (*reading, slowly, from the open book on the small table in front of her*) "And she who is struck dumb, when she speak, then will the spell be cast, and the horror grow in the place where the deed was done. In the depths of the night, after the murder has been done . . . in the dark, the sound of footsteps that have never walked the earth . . . the walking of dead feet . . . the moving of dead lips . . . the waving of dead hands . . ."

MRS WRAGG (*sitting at the head of the supper-table, her back to the footlights, moaning*) Don't—don't . . .

MRS ARTHUR. "In the depths of the night, the heart that ceases to beat . . ." (*In an hysterical whisper*) Let me go . . . Let me go . . .

(*She stumbles past the sofa and clings weakly to the left proscenium arch.* BEATRICE *makes to follow her.* JIMMY *holds her back*)

JIMMY (*to Beatrice; after a pause*) It's no use . . . When we decided to try—this, I don't think we quite realized—what we were getting mixed up in. It may end in anything. It may end in —death for all of us. It's something ordinary brains and ordinary courage can't fight.

BEATRICE. I know.

(JIMMY *takes a key from his wallet*)

That's the key of the stage door. What are you doing?

(JIMMY *gives one last look at the Woman, and goes up to the alcove. He nerves himself for a last effort*)

No—no . . .

(*He wrenches the curtains open on the dead body. They recoil*)

JIMMY. And now I'm going to get the police.

BEATRICE (*rushing up to him, with a cry*) No, no! I know—I was a fool to start it. I was mad to cut that wire . . . But please don't go . . .
JIMMY. I must.
BEATRICE. I'm—I'm afraid of those corridors . . . You may never get to that door alive!

(*They are all getting beyond control.* THE WOMAN *sits motionless in their midst*)

JIMMY. I must, for all of us . . .
MRS ARTHUR. For God's sake go! Fetch the police . . .
BEATRICE. I forbid you to leave this stage . . .
MRS ARTHUR. We must get help! We must! We must!
MISS GROZE. If he doesn't we shall all be killed.
MRS ARTHUR. Please go . . .
MISS GROZE. Please—please go . . .
MRS WRAGG (*with a sudden cry*) Look! (*She rises*)

(*The babel is silent.* THE WOMAN *has risen. A strange look, as if awakening, lights up her face.* BEATRICE *moves slowly down to her.* THE WOMAN *crosses her hands. They seem to intertwine again, and make signs, as if she were trying to tell them something. Silence*)

BEATRICE. Would you like to write down what you want to tell us?
THE WOMAN (*suddenly*) Why have you brought me here?

(*They gasp and shrink away from her. A pause. Muffled knocking upstairs*)

BEATRICE. Close that curtain!

(JIMMY *closes the curtain over the dead body*)

THE WOMAN. Where am I?
JIMMY. You're on the stage of a London theatre.
THE WOMAN. Which—London theatre?
JIMMY. The St James's.
THE WOMAN (*with a start*) Is this a trap?

(*They look at one another*)

JIMMY. You walked in here, half an hour ago.
THE WOMAN. But why didn't you question me?
JIMMY. We waited for you to speak . . .
THE WOMAN. And what did I say?
JIMMY. Nothing. You were making—signs.
THE WOMAN. Signs?
JIMMY. As if you were—dumb.
THE WOMAN. Dumb? (*Incredulously*) Dumb? (*With the sudden realization of terror*) Dumb! And this is the St James's Theatre! Tell me it's not true! Tell me you're playing a joke! You are,

aren't you? It isn't really the night-time, is it? You've just closed
the shutters and lit the candles, haven't you? Just to frighten me
all the more! Tell me it's daylight!

BEATRICE. It is—the night-time . . .

THE WOMAN (*moving away from her, shaking her head*) It isn't, it
isn't . . . And this isn't the St James's Theatre . . . Why, the next
thing you'll be telling me is that there's a dead body behind that
curtain!

(*They start. She sees them*)

It is the night-time . . . This is the St James's Theatre . . . (*Sitting
by the supper-table, dully*) And there's a dead body behind that
curtain . . .

(*A pause*)

BEATRICE. Won't you—tell us how you got here?

THE WOMAN. I was on my way to a séance . . .

BEATRICE. A séance?

THE WOMAN. For black magic . . .

(*They shrink. She rises and crosses to Beatrice like a guilty child*)

I've tried to give it up, God knows I've tried! But my grandfather
practised it, I know, and his mother was burnt at the stake at
Hereford . . .

BEATRICE. Burnt?

THE WOMAN (*sitting in the armchair, sullenly*) As a witch . . .
The séance was round the corner from here. I got out of my car
in Piccadilly, and walked down, and then I stood on the pave-
ment near this theatre. It was about ten o'clock.

JIMMY. Ten o'clock . . .

THE WOMAN. I was looking at a poster. Yes, I can remember.
It said, "This theatre is closed." I could hear the noise of the
traffic . . . And the lights . . . I remember distinctly.

BEATRICE. Yes?

THE WOMAN. I felt a hand on my shoulder.

BEATRICE. Yes?

THE WOMAN. I turned round . . . There was nobody there.
There was nobody there, but—there was a hand on my shoulder!

BEATRICE. What do you mean?

THE WOMAN. A human hand . . . It ended at the wrist.

JIMMY (*in a whisper*) Good God!

THE WOMAN. The light and the noise of the traffic just faded
away . . . That's the last I remember.

BEATRICE. What—sort of a hand?

THE WOMAN. It had a signet ring—with initials . . . Let me see
. . . Yes . . . Yes . . . I've nearly got them.

BEATRICE. Yes?

THE WOMAN (*with great effort*) C—J . . . (*She rests her head on her hand, with a sigh, and her eyes fall on the open book on the table beside her)* Why, there they are! At the end of this chapter!

BEATRICE. Charles—Jasper . . .

THE WOMAN. Charles Jasper! *(Urgently)* He wrote this book, didn't he? I know all about it! I know all about this theatre! Tell me the truth! Has there—been a—murder here?

(A pause)

JIMMY. Yes.

BEATRICE. Don't—don't get frightened . . . We're all in just as much danger as you are . . .

THE WOMAN. No, you're not! . . . Why couldn't I speak to you when I came in? I've never been dumb in my life. And it says in that book—that a dumb woman will be found . . . *(Suddenly terrified)* Oh, what is going to happen to me? What is going to happen to me?

JIMMY. Nothing—nothing!

BEATRICE. Of course not!

JIMMY *(turning to the archway)* I'm going to get help . . .

BEATRICE. You can't!

JIMMY. I must! Don't you see? God knows what's between here and the stage door of this theatre, but something's got to be done . . .

BEATRICE. I know you'd never get to the door alive . . .

JIMMY *(running across to the right proscenium)* Then I'll try through the front of the theatre.

BEATRICE *(after him, entreatingly)* It's all locked up! And it's dark! No, no . . . We've all got to be together, whatever happens. Only on the other side of those walls there are crowds, and lights, and life, and here we are, locked up with darkness and—death . . .

THE WOMAN. You're frightened too.

(They turn to her again)

Why do you look at me like that? You look as if I were going to decide . . . Perhaps the book will tell me what I ought to do. *(She takes the book from the table)*

BEATRICE. No! No! *(She forces the book from the Woman)*

THE WOMAN. Let me have it, please!

BEATRICE *(passing it quickly to Jimmy)* It's a stupid book!

THE WOMAN. You were thinking of your own safety only a second ago. Why you are so concerned about me, all of a sudden? *(Rising, and turning from one face to the other)* Why are you all looking at me?

(They cannot answer)

(Creeping across to Jimmy, her tone changing) There's something in that book you're trying to hide from me! *(She snatches the book from*

him and sits by the supper-table. She turns over the pages in a fever of impatience)

BEATRICE (*falling to her knees before her*)   Throw it away! I beg you to throw it away!

THE WOMAN. What's this underlined?

BEATRICE. On my knees I pray you to throw that book away . . .

THE WOMAN. What's this underlined? (*Reading slowly*) "And she—who is struck dumb, when she speak, then will the spell be cast, and the horror grow in the place where the deed was done . . ."

MRS ARTHUR. Don't go on!

THE WOMAN (*reading*)   "And when she speak, then will she be called to her death . . ." (*She looks at the others as if she had not understood what she said. She turns to the book again and goes on reading*) "And on her dead body will rise the ghost of the murdered." (*She puts the book down on the table, and looks at the others*) And there's been a murder done here tonight. And I was struck dumb . . . Let me go . . .

JIMMY. But you can go, if you like . . . Here's the key of the stage door . . . Once you're in the street you'll have nothing to fear!

(*She rises. They watch her. Slowly, she sits again*)

THE WOMAN. I can't go . . . I'm frightened to move. (*Realizing it suddenly*) You said, once I'm in the street I'll have nothing to fear . . .

JIMMY. Absolutely nothing.

THE WOMAN. That means that in here—I have everything to fear . . . Doesn't it?

(*They quail before her look*)

(*Half crying*) You will look after me, won't you?

JIMMY. Of course we will.

THE WOMAN. Are you sure?

JIMMY. Of course we're sure!

(THE WOMAN *gives a sigh of relief and lets her head fall on the table. A pause. She lifts her head. She is staring at the lower end of the table, where stands the stool that has been empty all the evening. A pause*)

BEATRICE. What is it?

THE WOMAN. Will you get up, please?

MRS ARTHUR. What—what is it?

THE WOMAN. Please ask him to get up.

BEATRICE. But—we can't see anything . . .

THE WOMAN. I know you can't. Because he's hiding behind the table . . . Is he afraid too?

MRS WRAGG. But there's nobody—behind the table . . .
THE WOMAN. But there's his hand. On the edge of the table.
BEATRICE. His hand! Where?
THE WOMAN (*pointing*) There! And he's wearing a signet ring!
BEATRICE. Oh . . .
THE WOMAN (*rising*) You're not making fun of me, are you?
You can see him, can't you?

(*They shake their heads. She moves forward, and looks in front of the table*)

BEATRICE (*breathlessly*) Well?
THE WOMAN. There's nobody . . .
JIMMY. Of course not!
THE WOMAN. But—the hand is still there!

(*They stare at her*)

Can't—can't you see it?

(*She looks imploringly from one to the other.* BEATRICE *crosses and buries her head in Mrs Wragg's shoulder*)

(*Tragically*) Then I'm alone. I'm cut off from you all . . . (*Clinging to the armchair, moaning, her eyes fixed on the supper-table*) Help me. No, I'm alone . . . (*With a sudden cry*) It's moving! Help me! Help me! It's coming . . . (*Retreating past the sofa*) Help me! Help me! It's following me! (*Her arms outstretched*) Help! Help . . .

(*Her shrieks die suddenly away. Her arms drop limply to her sides. She looks at her own right shoulder, and seems to watch something lift up her right arm as if to guide her. She is again under the spell that was over her before she spoke.*
As if drawn by an unseen force, she walks out through the archway and is swallowed up in the darkness out of which she came. Silence. JIMMY *walks fearfully to the archway and looks out into the darkness. He turns to the others, his hands clenched*)

JIMMY (*quietly*) Listen to me . . .
MISS GROZE (*with a cry*) He's terrified himself! He's terrified himself!
JIMMY (*loudly*) Listen to me! I am terrified . . . We're up against something I never knew existed. And we're locked up with it, between the four walls of this theatre. We've got to face it . . . It may kill us. I don't know. We can't do anything. (*He considers a moment*) He—mustn't find—her . . . (*He turns to the archway*)
BEATRICE. Where are you going?
JIMMY. I'm going to see—where she is.

(JIMMY *vanishes into the darkness*)

BEATRICE (*turning to the others, with new courage*) He's right.

We've got to keep our heads. Don't think of what you may see happening in front of your eyes ... Think of sunshine—crowds —anything.

(*Louder knocking upstairs*)

MRS ARTHUR. He'll burst open that door!

BEATRICE (*with terrific insistence*) We've got to—keep him— there ...

(JIMMY *returns, a look of fixed horror on his face. He turns round twice, to look back into the darkness. He sinks on a stool by the supper-table, staring in front of him, dazed. They wait*)

JIMMY. She's lying over there, half-way down the stairs ... He won't see her there ... Her heart had just—stopped.

(*They shudder.* MRS WRAGG *sinks on a stool*)

(*In a dead voice*) Sudden fright ... She saw something. Her face was terribly—twisted. (*He rises and recovers himself*) Mrs Wragg, somebody, quite soon, may want to jump over the footlights and get away in the dark ... I want you to be in this corner—you'll be quite safe there—and let down the safety curtain ...

MRS WRAGG (*almost in tears*) I daren't, sir, I daren't ...

BEATRICE. Mrs Wragg—you'll be quite safe! (*Crossing, and putting her arms about her*) I promise you.

MRS WRAGG. All right, my dear, all right ...

JIMMY. And we're all here ... Every one of us ...

(*Loud knocking upstairs*)

Except Mullins. We've got to keep our heads, remember ...

(*Suddenly, without any warning,* MISS GROZE *collapses in a heap against the sofa.* JIMMY *rushes down to her*)

BEATRICE. She's seen something—out there ...

(*She crosses fearfully, clinging to Mrs Wragg. They are all huddled round the sofa, in the left corner of the stage*)

What—what did you see?

MISS GROZE (*raising her head, weakly*) There's somebody— standing—out there!

(*Terror grips at their hearts*)

JIMMY. But—but we're all here ...

MRS ARTHUR. It's somebody come in from the street!

JIMMY. Everywhere's locked up. Nobody can have come in from the street ...

MRS ARTHUR. There's only Mullins in the theatre. It must have been Mullins!

(Loud knocking upstairs. Their hearts are little more than still)

BEATRICE. It—isn't—Mullins . . .

JIMMY. And we're all here . . .

BEATRICE *(with a cry)* Look!

(A faint and mysterious grey light has grown in the darkness beyond the archway. It fades slowly away.

Out of the darkness slowly and noiselessly appears the shape of a man. It is the ghost of CHARLES JASPER. He is wearing his dinner-jacket, and looks exactly as he did, except that he is very pale and bears on his face a look of extraordinary calm. He walks slowly down the stage, and sits on the stool at the foot of the supper-table, his back to the footlights, his hands folded on the table before him. He has made no sound of any kind, neither has he looked at any of the others. A pause. Knocking upstairs)

Remember, it will need the biggest courage you've ever shown anywhere . . . Now *(clasping Jimmy by the arm)* go and unlock the door and let him out.

(JIMMY goes out to the right of the archway. A pause, while they muster up courage. They cross, all together, their faces averted fearfully, and take their places at the table. MRS WRAGG, at a signal from BEATRICE, takes a bottle of champagne from the bucket beside her and begins to pour out)

JIMMY *(off)* I'm frightfully sorry . . .

(He comes back, followed immediately by MULLINS. MRS WRAGG retreats into the background)

The catch must have slipped . . .

MULLINS *(savagely, a little intoxicated)* Well, it was distinctly annoying. Didn't you hear me knock several times?

JIMMY *(coming down backwards, and standing so as to hide the foot of the table from Mullins)* Only once, and I came straight up.

BEATRICE. I'm so sorry, Mr Mullins.

MULLINS. And I've seen thousands of photographs, but not one of my charming hostess as Juliet.

BEATRICE. I'm so sorry.

MULLINS *(looking at his watch)* It's just on eleven! *(Sneering)* Where can Sir Charles be, Lady Jasper?

(BEATRICE rises and goes to him with a glass of champagne)

BEATRICE. Won't you drink my husband's health with us?

MULLINS *(taking the glass from her, ironically)* Certainly, Lady Jasper . . .

(BEATRICE sits again. He looks again at his watch)

I wonder if my watch is right . . .

BEATRICE (*calmly and clearly*) Is it the right time—Charles?

(*Silence. Slowly* MULLINS'S *head turns, and his eyes travel to the group round the table. They rest at last on the dark figure at the end. He gives a violent start*)

Charles is very sorry, Mr Mullins, but he fell asleep—over a glass of wine.

(*A pause.* MULLINS *is still staring*)

JIMMY (*unsteadily*) And now, I think, is the moment to drink to our host . . . To Sir Charles Jasper!

(*The others rise. They are about to drink when the clock begins to strike eleven. They listen, their glasses in the air, brimming with wine.* MULLINS, *in a blaze of fury, dashes his glass to the floor*)

MULLINS. I won't drink! (*Beside himself, turning on the figure sitting at the foot of the table, perfectly still*) You've beaten me! But even if you have, I've been damn clever all the same! And you'll try and stop them knowing how clever I was, will you? By pretending nothing at all happened, will you? You're going to be kind to me and let me off, are you? You're going to forgive me? Forgive me! That clock striking now means two million pounds have slipped through my fingers, but you won't stop me telling them how near I came to your blasted two million! (*He tears from a pocket a page of manuscript and tosses it on the table*) That's my short story! Look! That's where I started dictating to him! That's how I got him to write his own suicide letter, when he wasn't committing suicide at all! And if that damn poison had worked, it would have come off, too! I've lost your two million like any common bungler, by not making sure you were dead when I left you—but I won't have you pretend I wasn't damn clever! Damn clever! Damn clever! Damn clever! Damn . . .!

(*His voice suddenly dies.* THE MAN *has turned his head, and is looking him between the eyes.*
THE MAN *rises and walks slowly across the stage.* MULLINS *steps back and watches, bewildered.* THE MAN *seems to melt slowly into the black curtains over the alcove. A pause.* JIMMY *walks to the alcove*)

BEATRICE. No—no . . .

(JIMMY *wrenches the curtains apart. The dead body lies in the armchair.* MULLINS *stares, quite uncomprehending. Then, suddenly, he leaps to the curtains and tears them together*)

MULLINS (*hysterical*) You didn't see that! You didn't see that!

You didn't see that! You didn't see that—there's nothing there! Look! There's nothing there! There's nothing there—look!

(*He tears back the curtains again. The dead body . . . He stares quite motionless for a moment, then gives a long scream of terror. He totters and collapses. A loud clanging noise, high above. He looks up*)

(*Duly*) What's that coming down?

(*The* SAFETY CURTAIN *begins to fall, slowly and implacably*)

It's a wall . . . A prison wall! . . . (*Falling to his knees, in a crescendo of madness*) Shutting me in! Shutting me in . . . Shutting me in . . .

The safety curtain will not rise again. But it need not. A murder has been arranged; a murder has taken place; and the murderer has been brought to book. The evening's adventure in the St James's Theatre, London, is over.

THE END

GROUND PLAN

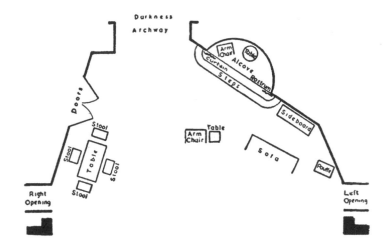

MADE AND PRINTED IN GREAT BRITAIN BY
LATIMER TREND & COMPANY LTD PLYMOUTH
MADE IN ENGLAND

Lightning Source UK Ltd.
Milton Keynes UK
UKOW06f0925130915

258536UK00012B/152/P